Jean Georges d'Hoste

# ALL VERSAILLES

*Preface by*
### *DANIEL MEYER*
*Chief Curator of the Musée National*
*des Châteaux de Versailles et de Trianon*

## 185 Colour illustrations

*Photographic service by*
### *GIANNI DAGLI ORTI*

**FB**
**BONECHI**

## FIRST FLOOR

1 — THE ROYAL CHAPEL
2 — THE OPERA ROYAL

3 — SALON D'HERCULE
4 — SALON DE L'ABONDANCE
5 — SALON DE VÉNUS
6 — SALON DE DIANE
7 — SALON DE MARS
8 — SALON DE MERCURE
9 — SALON D'APOLLON

10 — SALON DE LA GUERRE
11 — THE HALL OF MIRRORS
12 — SALON DE LA PAIX

13 — THE QUEEN'S BEDCHAMBER
14 — LA MÉRIDIENNE
15 — BIBLIOTHÈQUE
16 — THE QUEEN'S PRIVATE ROOMS
17 — SALON DES NOBLES
18 — ANTICHAMBRE DE LA REINE
19 — THE GUARD ROOM

20 — SALLE DU SACRE
21 — SALLE DE 1792
22 — ESCALIER DES PRINCES
23 — THE GALLERY OF THE BATTLES

* 24 — THE GUARD ROOM
25 — SALON DU GRAND COUVERT
26 — SALON DE L'ŒIL-DE-BŒUF
27 — THE KING'S CHAMBER
28 — THE COUNCIL HALL

* 29 — PETITE CHAMBRE DU ROI
30 — CABINET DE LA PENDULE
31 — CABINET DES CHIENS
32 — DEGRÉ DU ROI
33 — SALLE À MANGER DES RETOURS DE CHASSE
34 — THE KING'S PRIVATE STUDY
35 — ARRIÈRE CABINET
36 — PIÈCE DE LA VAISSELLE D'OR
37 — LOUIS XVI'S LIBRARY
38 — THE PORCELAIN ROOM
39 — BILLARD
40 — THE KING'S GAMING ROOM

## GROUND-FLOOR

**THE DAUPHIN'S APARTMENT**
1 — 1ère ANTICHAMBRE DE LA DAUPHINE
2 — 2nde ANTICHAMBRE DE LA DAUPHINE
3 — GRAND CABINET DE LA DAUPHINE
4 — CHAMBRE DE LA DAUPHINE
5 — CABINET INTÉRIEUR DE LA DAUPHINE
6 — BIBLIOTHÈQUE DU DAUPHIN
7 — GRAND CABINET DU DAUPHIN
8 — CHAMBRE DU DAUPHIN
9 — 2nde ANTICHAMBRE DU DAUPHIN
10 — 1ère ANTICHAMBRE DU DAUPHIN
11 — SALLE DES GARDES DU DAUPHIN

**MARIE ANTOINETTE'S GROUND FLOOR APARTMENT**
12 — CHAMBRE DE LA REINE
13 — VESTIBULE LOUIS XIII
14 — SALLE DE BAIN DE LA REINE

**THE ROOMS OF THE DAUGHTERS OF FRANCE**
15 — 1ère ANTICHAMBRE DE MADAME VICTOIRE
16 — SALON DES NOBLES DE MADAME VICTOIRE
17 — GRAND CABINET DE MADAME VICTOIRE
18 — CHAMBRE DE MADAME VICTOIRE
19 — CABINET INTÉRIEUR DE MADAME VICTOIRE
20 — BIBLIOTHÈQUE DE MADAME VICTOIRE
21 — CABINET INTÉRIEUR DE MADAME ADELAÏDE
22 — CHAMBRE DE MADAME ADELAÏDE
23 — GRAND CABINET DE MADAME ADELAÏDE

24 — THE STAIRCASE LOUIS PHILIPPE
25 — THE ROOM HOQUETONS

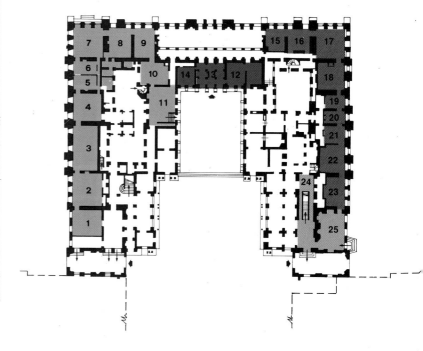

*Guided visit*

# PREFACE

Versailles, nowadays, has become what might be called a Museum-Palace. A Museum because it is no longer inhabited, at least not in the principal parts; Palace because it was originally planned as a dwelling. On closer study Versailles is actually a Palace and a Museum, one as well as the other, depending on what part of the building is involved. It was first and foremost a palace: the country residence for Louis XIII and the young XIV, governmental headquarters and principal residence for Louis XIV when he was older, for Louis XV and for Louis XVI. The Revolution of 1789 and the forced return of the Royal Family to Paris on October 6th of that year meant the end of life in a place that had been what dreams are made of for a little over a hundred years. After the Revolution nothing, not even the attempts of Napoleon I and Louis XVIII and the work they had carried out, succeeded in reanimating it.

It initiated its second vocation as Museum when Louis Philippe realized that the only way to save the palace from abandon was to dedicate it to all the Glories of France. At the risk of destroying various exquisite aspects of the mansions of the Bourbon kings, his ancestors, the man who was known as the Citizen-king made Versailles the first portrait museum in the world and the most important Museum of French History.

As time passed, feelings gradually abated and at the beginning of the 20th century the Curators attempted to turn back the clock and bit by bit have succeeded in fusing the two separate concepts of Museum and Château into a single whole, that of Museum-Palace, in other words of a Palace undoubtedly transformed into a Museum, but still able to show the descendents of those who drove out the legitimate masters what the life of the great sovereigns who marked the apogee of their nation was like.

As chance would have it, the late 17th century and the 18th century were the most glorious periods for the decorative arts in France. One is therefore tempted to search for the furniture and reweave the hangings and tapestries which decorated the apartments of the French kings. Is it really feasible? Only in part, for so much was lost in Revolutionary times when it was sold. Is it auspicable? It is not our place to pass judgement on those charged with the task of rearrangement.

The danger exists of neglecting the rooms consecrated to our history, which are certainly no longer what they were when the Museum was created in 1837, except for an occasional strong point such as the Gallery of the Battles. The public is eager for precision but at the same time it wants to dream. And precision will be found in the chronological succession of what were once known as the Historical Galleries. Yet it can also dream as it wanders through the apartments hoping to run into the Sun King in the Gallery of Mirrors or Marie Antoinette in the Petite-Trianon.

The visitor therefore needs a guide in order to understand all the aspects of such a vast dwelling. It is difficult to realize a text where an equal amount of space is allotted to the photos and the comments. Jean Georges d'Hoste has succeeded in having the images and descriptions go hand in hand. He has also seen to it that extensive explanations are available, for which we are grateful, as in the case of the Gallery of the Battles where, almost always, the painting is explained in its anecdotal context. We are also grateful for the fact that he at times insisted on furnishing the origin of certain words, such as the Dauphin, or for having provided brief chronological or geneological notes which justify the state of the apartments. Lastly we are also obliged to him for having underscored the fact that in the lapse of time between the writing of the book and its publication changes in the exhibitions may have taken place.

All these qualities are why we hope the album for which we have the pleasure to write this preface will live up to the expectations of the various categories of "public" who crowd in throughout the year to enter what is left of the most marvellous palace ever created.

DANIEL MEYER
Chief Curator of the Musée National
des Châteaux de Versailles et de Trianon

3

Left. Above: Versailles around 1664 by Adam-François van der Meulen. Below: view of Versailles and the gardens in 1668 by Pierre Patel.

The palace in 1772 in a painting by Pierre-Denis Martin.

# WHEN KINGS LIVED IN VERSAILLES

*Versailles. The world over this name evokes visions of a glittering court. Henry IV, who went hunting in these lands, and his son, Louis XIII, who had a hunting lodge built here, could never have imagined that this was the beginning of one of the most famous monuments in France.*

*A great hunter like all the Bourbons, Louis XIII gradually bought up the lands around the pavilion and then in 1631 he took over the entire estate of the Gondi family which had come from Florence with the retinue of Catherine de' Medici.*

*Later the king had the original building restructured into a small château in stone and brick surrounded by a moat.*

*The palace we now see developed around this nucleus. Louis XIII died*

*in 1643 and for almost twenty years no thought was given to new buildings or remodeling. Young Louis XIV occasionally went hunting here and brought along his mistress, Louise de la Vallière, with a small entourage of friends. Finally in 1661 construction work that was to continue for a good part of his long reign was begun. The internal transformations were followed by a general restructuration in 1666.*

*The minister Colbert had for some time been preparing the downfall of the superintendent of finance Fouquet whose arrest after the extraordinary fete of Vaux, on August 17, 1661, was not at all a direct result of the envy of a king who had been humbled by such a show of luxury and ostentation. The greatest names*

*of the time had been called in to make this mansion all the more resplendent: Le Vau, Le Brun, Le Nôtre, Molière, La Fontaine, Scarron... all artists who were thereafter also to be found in Versailles.*

*Some reprove Louis XIV for his megalomania and unlimited pride. We rather believe though that the young king had a political scope as well as economic ends in mind as the idea of the château of Versailles shaped up. He never forgot la Fronde who made him sleep on the straw in the cold and empty castle of Saint-Germain. He never forgot this final act of rebellion of the large landholders and he decided to keep these disturbing elements at bay. What he needed to attract and "keep watch" over them, was a fine château.*

5

On the other hand he loved this land of Versailles. He was young and he took his métier de Roi seriously and considered his country the most beautiful of all.

The first thing to do in giving concrete form to this idea of greatness was to forego foreign commissions which did nothing but bleed the French treasury white. From Francis I to Mazarin, France had imported art works and artists, above all from Italy. Preference was now given to works of French origin and its diffusion was so widespread that for a long time France was synonymous with good taste.

All of France worked for Versailles. At the king's behest various Académies were created to stimulate a real true rebirth of French art. For example, the mirrors in the Grand Gallery were produced by the Royal Mirror Factory, founded by Colbert in 1665 and then installed in the factory of Saint-Gobain. In 1667 a royal edict for the reorganization of the Gobelins was promulgated and Louis XIV organized exhibitions of the products in the Appartement. The marble quarries of Saint-Béat in

the Pyrrhenees, abandoned in Roman times, were reopened and are still producing. Louis XV on the other hand exhibited the production of the porcelain factories of Vincennes and Sèvres in his private rooms, personally promoting the sales. By making large orders for the queen he also relaunched the activity of the Lyon silk weaving establishments which were in difficulty.

But let's go back to the beginning. The number of workers employed at the château was considerable. In 1683 there were 30,000. Dangeau in his Diary, dated May 31, 1685, mentions 36,000. But there were never enough and the king was forced to entrust some of the excavation and earth removal, including the Orangerie and the pool, to his troops.

Throughout Louis XIV's reign the construction yards multiplied and the king as well as his reluctant courtiers learned to live with dust and noise. Le Nôtre set to work. The king wanted a fine park - and in 1664 it was ready for the fete of the Plaisirs de l'île enchantée in honor of Mademoiselle de la Vallière. Le Vau enveloped Louis XVII's brick château

and created two projecting bodies overlooking the garden and inserted an "Italian" terrace which was later to be the site of the Hall of Mirrors. Le Vau died in 1670 and work was continued by his pupil, François Dorbay. He in turn was succeeded in 1678 by Hardouin-Mansart who had become first architect to the

Left: Louis XV, by Pierre-Adrien Gois (1731-1823). "The most handsome man in France" strikes a pose.

Right: Louis XVI, by Jean-Antoine Houdon (1741-1828). This bust reveals the outstanding aspects of the king's character: inherent goodness but also indolence, indecision and a certain bitterness. Qualities and defects of a simple man which will provide the Revolution with a pretext.

king. Le Brun was charged with the interior decoration. Colbert, ever ready to have his say, protested but then laid out the money. The South Wing (1678-1682) and the North Wing (1685-1689) were built. Work began on the Salon de l'Opera only in 1768-1769.

The greatest obstacle to overcome was the supply of water for the fountains with their 1,400 jets which use 62,000 hectoliters of water per hour. Water from the river Bièvre was brought in by an aqueduct but soon proved insufficient. Water from various ponds was then used and reservoirs were built. The water engineers invented a thousand contraptions and finally Marly's machine was created. Not even this was enough and the king had new projects which would use the waters of the Seine undertaken. This project was shelved and its place was taken by another one in which the waters of the Eure were to be used. But the enormous amount of work involved proved too much and the undertaking came to a halt.

At the end of his reign Louis XIV could well be satisfied with what he had done: he had offered France the most beautiful palace in the world. His successors made no great changes, aside from the considerable remodelling done inside.

The Revolution was at the gates. On October 5, 1789, the people of Paris marched on Versailles, invaded the palace and took the royal family back to the capital. In 1793 after the fall of the monarchy the furnishings of the palace were sold at auction and the works of art were transferred to the Louvre.

Napoleon never liked Versailles. The palace gradually fell into ruin. The father of the painter Delacroix was of the opinion that it should be demolished and plowed under. Then Louis Philippe ordered it to be restored, paying in part out of his own pocket, and turning it over to the country as a historical museum. During the war of 1870 it was occupied by the Germans, after which it became the seat of the National Assembly until 1879.

After World War I the contributions of a wealthy American patron rescued the palace.

Since then the curators have in turn done all they could to restore part of its past to Versailles.

Versailles also represents the history of the French people. Every structure, every ornament, piece of furniture or tapestry tells us about the men who gave their all in building this palace dedicated "A toutes les Gloires de la France".

*Play of light and shade on the gates and the facades of the palace.*

*The equestrian statue of Louis XIV welcomes visitors at the entrance.*

**Versailles today** - The imposing mole of the palace, with its countless galleries, rooms of state, private apartments, and gardens and, of course, the two Trianons, unquestionably requires a certain amount of time if one wants to obtain more than a superficial idea of the palace of the last kings of France.

The Museum Administration has arranged for a variety of tours and itineraries. At any one time some of the rooms may however be closed - for maintenance, reordering or restoration - or they may only be open in turn.

In our guide we have tried to adhere to a logical order which will not necessarily be that required by the visit to the rooms. We have in any case included practically everything that can be visited.

In the light of new studies or new acquisitions the Direction of the Museum may of course decide to move individual paintings, furniture or objects so that they will provide a better picture of the surroundings in which life at court took place. Our readers are therefore requested not to be surprised at any changes they may encounter.

We are however certain that the visit will be interesting and profitable and that our book, dedicated to clarity and precision, will be a valid aid to all.

*Above: the vestibule on the ground floor of the Royal Chapel.* Louis XIV Crossing the Rhine, *by Coustou. Facing page: the Royal Chapel.*

# THE ROYAL CHAPEL

From the Royal Court we enter the palace on the right and find ourselves in an ample vestibule decorated with Ionic columns. In front of us is the bas-relief by Nicolas and Guillaume Coustou representing Louis XIV crossing the Rhine. The large door on the right leads into the Royal Chapel.

This chapel, dedicated to Saint Louis, was begun in the year 1700 by Jules Hardouin-Mansart (1646-1708), one of the most brilliant architects of the time. He came from a family of builders and was the son of a painter. When he was 29 he was elected to the Académie and soon became First Architect and Superintendent of Building. Basically he was responsible for Versailles as we see it now. He built this chapel not far from the preceding chapel, in the upper part of which the Hall of Hercules had been installed. He recruited the best artists of the time as collaborators: the sculptors Nico-

las and Guillaume Coustou, Laurent Magnier, René Frémin, François Antoine Vassé, the painter François Lemoyne, all part of the art world which was then coming to the fore in France.

Although the architect proposed the use of polychrome marble, the king preferred a fine white stone from the quarries of Créteil. The large wide windows lend a marvelous almost surrealistic luminosity to the architectural complex. While the massive pillars of the ground floor are decorated with angels bearing the attributes of the Passion and cult objects, the first floor is cadenced by elegant grooved Corinthian columns which support the trabeation on which the vaulted ceiling rests. The frescoes of the vault representing *God the Father Announcing the Coming of the Messiah* are by Antoine Coypel (1661-1722) and in the painter's search for expression reveal the influence of Le Brun as

well as of Italian art. The architecture of the vault is decorated with paintings by Philippe Meusnier, a specialist in this genre.

Above the altar, in the apse conch, is the *Resurrection of Christ* by Charles de Lafosse (1636-1716), a pupil of Le Brun, who spent some time in Italy and in particular Venice, where he acquired his taste for color and movement which safeguarded him from becoming too academic.

The ostentatious gilded bronze fixtures glowing on the altar are by Corneille Van Clève (1645-1732) while the organ case is by Robert Cliquot, one of the most notable of the French organ makers. The pavement is covered by polychrome marble in large designs. The royal coat of arms is at the center of the nave.

A spiral staircase leads to the first floor. The king and queen attended the service from projecting balconies in the tribune - the king on the left and the queen on the right. The ladies took their places in the gallery and the courtiers on the ground floor. All of them followed the mass facing the king. Louis XIV, who was very devoted, demanded a serious demeanor and silence. The service must have seemed interminable to the ladies who came above all in the hopes of drawing the king's attention. One day Brissac, head of the Guards, announced that the king would not attend mass that day. Almost all the ladies present immediately left, but it was a joke and when the king arrived, he was surprised to find the chapel empty...

Hardouin-Mansart died in 1708 and his place was taken by his brother-in-law Robert de Cotte, who brought work on the chapel to its end and it was inaugurated on June 5, 1710. Shortly thereafter, on July 7th, the first grand wedding was celebrated there with all the court present - that of the Duc de Berry, the king's nephew, with Mademoiselle, daughter of the Duc d'Orléans. Among the other royal weddings mention should be made of that of the Dauphin Louis, Louis XV's son, who never mounted the throne, and of his sons, the future king Louis XVI with Marie Antoinette of Austria on a lovely spring day, May 16, 1770; the Comte de Provence, the future Louis XVIII, with Louise of Savoy, in 1771, and in 1773, the wedding of the Comte d'Artois, the future Charles X, last king of France, with Maria Theresa of Savoy.

This chapel was also where the Knights of the Order of the Holy Ghost organized their great ceremonies and where the Te Deums were sung in thanks for victories. The Royal Chapel is therefore the site of the great religious events of the French monarchy.

*Above:* God the Father Announcing the Coming of the Messiah to the World, *detail of the frescoes in the vault.*
*Below: the high altar and the imposing decoration in bronze by Van Clève.*
*On the opposite page: the frescoes by Coypel in the vault.*

# THE OPÉRA ROYAL

Not until Louis XV were musical performances provided with a suitable setting. And what a setting it was! Commissioned from Ange Jacques Gabriel (1698-1782), the hall took only 21 months to build and it was ready to be inaugurated on the occasion of the wedding of the Dauphin Louis, the future Louis XVI.

The first opera theater in oval form, it was built entirely of wood, painted in faux marble, which gives it perfect acoustics, and with a capacity of 750 spectators who crowded in for concerts or operas. King Louis XV spurned a large royal box for three small boxes closed by a grate. Thanks to an exceptional device, the pit could be lifted to the level of the stage, after which the orchestra pit was covered and the room could be transformed into an elegant ballroom or banquet hall. The stage, the largest in France after that of the Paris Opéra which was built a century later, is 26 meters deep and 22 meters wide.

The wooden decoration was by the hand of the sculptor Augustin Pajou (1730-1809).

The canvas which still decorates the ceiling was painted by Louis-Jean-Jacques Durameau (1733-1798), painter to the king who had become curator of the paintings of the Crown in 1783. It represents *Apollo Offering a Laurel Crown to Men Who Have Distinguished Themselves in the Arts.*

The last banquet was organized in this room on October 2, 1789, in honor of the regiment of Flanders which Louis XVI had called in to protect the palace and its inhabitants. But all to no avail for the Revolution swept away the regiment, the guards, the carpets, mirrors, furniture... In 1871 the room was the seat of the National Assembly: the walls, already in a state of disrepair in the time of Louis Philippe, were whitewashed and Durameau's canvas was detached and placed at the back of the stage, so that a window might be put in its place. In 1952 an integral restoration was begun, bringing back to light the glitter of gold and the pink and blue tones of this unique room in which everything harmonizes perfectly, from the chandeliers to the curtain embroidered in gold with the king's coat of arms.

The cost of the spectacles was however prohibitive. As many as 3,000 candles were required just to illuminate the hall and it was therefore used as little as possible. It was sporadically opened on the occasion of visits by foreign royalty, for grand gala balls, and French lyric operas, particularly Glück and Rameau.

*The interior of the Opéra Royal.*
*Facing page. Above, right: the royal box.*

# THE STATE APARTMENTS

**Salon d'Hercule** - Adjacent to the vestibule of the chapel this is the first salon to be encountered before entering the State Apartments. Robert de Cotte (1656-1735) began the decoration after finishing work on the chapel. Son, brother and, subsequently father, of renowned architects, Robert became architect to the king when he was only 31 and director of the Gobelin Factory ten years later. Under his direction the famous workshop which had been closed for seven years due to lack of funds reacquired the prestige it had in the time of Charles Le Brun, its former director.

The decoration of this large room reserved for receptions was continued in 1725 after various years of interruption. The visitor is immediately struck by the beauty of the red marble pilasters with capitals in gilded bronze which confer an air of courtly sumptuousness to the room. Over the fireplace is a painting by Veronese, *Eleazer and Rebecca*, accompanied by another of this Venetian painter's works, *Simon the Pharisee*, which covers the entire wall. Louis XIV greatly admired the Italian painters, in particular Veronese and Titian. The Venetian Republic gave him the latter work in 1664. But it is the ceiling which attracts our attention for the beauty of the paintings by François Lemoyne. The artist worked for 3 years on the decoration of this surface of 315 square meters and a few months later, worn out and exhausted, he took his life. The immense work represents the *Apotheosis of Hercules* with more than 140 figures subdivided into various groups representing the gods of Olympus, the *Vices* and the *Virtues*. From the summit of a cloud, Jupiter receives Hercules, who firmly grasps his club, and presents the hero with Hebe, the goddess of youth, as his bride. The other gods include Diana with the crescent moon, Venus, and the cupids which were mandatory at such a happy event.....

16

**Salon de l'Abondance** - Much smaller than the Salon d'Hercule, the Room of Plenty is the first of a series of six consecutive rooms in the State Apartments overlooking the Parterre to the north.

Some of Louis XIV's collections, now in the Louvre, were kept in this room which led to the *Cabinet of Medals and Curiosities* through the door across from the window. In the time of Louis XVI it became the king's gaming room. On the walls covered in green Genoa velvet hang the portraits of the Grand Dauphin, Louis XIV's son, and two of the Dauphin's sons - the Duc d'Anjou, who was to become king of Spain under the name of Philip V, and his brother the Duc de Bourgogne, father of Louis XV, painted by Rigaud. Another painting by J.-B. Van Loo is of Louis XV. The ceiling was decorated by René Antoine Houasse

(1645-1710), a pupil of Le Brun, employed more than once for the decorations of Versailles and the Trianon. The theme represented is that of *Royal Magnificence*, also found in monochrome gold on faux marble in a medallion over the door.

The two medallion showcases in ebony and brass enhanced by beautiful repoussé gilt bronze were made by Alexandre Jean Oppenordt (1639-1715). This French cabinetmaker worked for the Manufacture Royale des Gobelins and created ten pieces of furniture like this for the palace of Versailles. He was an emulator of André Charles Boulle (1642-1732) who created famous pieces in ebony decorated with tortoise and brass inlay. On either side of the doors, four busts in patinated bronze on tapered pedestals from the collections of the king.

18

*The Salon de Venus. On the opposite page: detail of the wainscotting (boiseries) with the emblem of the sun representing the power of the king and the royal scepter and the hand of justice.*

**The Salon de Vénus -** Originally this room served as antechamber to the State Apartments. It was at the head of the Ambassadors' Staircase which fell into disrepair. The radical restoration would have been so costly that in Louis XV's time it was torn down and replaced by another staircase which leads to the Hall of Hercules. On the ceiling, *Venus Crowned by the Graces* by Houasse. The Goddess of Love casts garlands of flowers around the gods at her feet: Mars, Vulcan, Bacchus, Neptune and Jupiter.

Famous couples are represented in the corners: Jason and Medea, Bacchus and Ariadne, Caesar and Cleopatra, Titus and Berenice. The central oval is continued by two monochrome paintings on a gilded ground: the *Rape of Europa* and *Amphitrite Towed by a Dolphin*. The vaults of the ceiling contain *Augustus and the Circensian Games*, *Nebuchadnezzar and Semiramis*, *Rossana and Alexander* and *Cyrus Preparing to Free a Maiden*.

In a niche on the back wall is a statue of Louis XIV by Jean Warin (1604-1672). The king, dressed as an ancient Roman, is surrounded by the attributes of war with shield, helmet and cuirass, and leans on the staff of command.

Two fine perspective views by Jacques Rousseau (1630-1693) decorate the side walls. Rousseau also painted the two trompe-l'œil statues in the area between the windows.

**Salon de Diane** - The first thing one notes upon entering this room is the bust of Louis XIV by Bernini. While the king had not liked Bernini's statue of him on horseback which he relegated to a secluded spot in the Orangerie, he certainly must have been pleased with this sculpture which portrayed him at the age of 27 with an intrepid resolute expression and with a loose fold of his clothing blown out by the wind over his left shoulder, giving the regal figure an air of youthful vitality.

The painting above the fireplace, *Iphigenia Carried Off by Diana*, is by Charles de Lafosse. Across from it is a delightful *Iphigenia Coming to See Endymion* by Gabriel Blanchard (1630-1704). On the ceiling *Diana Presiding Over the Hunt and Navigation* by Blanchard. The paintings in the vault, *Jason and the Argonauts* and *Alexander Hunting Lions* are by Charles de Lafosse while *Cyrus Hunting Boars* and *Caesar Sending a Roman Colony to Carthage* are by Claude Aubran (1639-1684).

This room was used as a billiard room, a game at which Louis XIV seems to have been particularly expert.

**Salon de Mars** - Used as a Guard Room, as befits its name, this room served as a Music Room in the evening. Audran painted *Mars on his Chariot* in the center of the ceiling, accompanied by *Victory Upheld by Hercules* by J. Jouvenet (1644-1717) and *Terror, Cruelty and Fear Mastering the Powers of the World* by Houasse. The coving is sumptuously decorated by Audran. Helmets and various warlike trophies are represented in the frieze under the cornice.

The Salon also contains various outstanding paintings: above the fireplace *King David* by Domenichino, originally in Louis XIV's chamber; to the left, the *Family of Darius* by Le Brun; to the right, the *Pilgrims of Emmaus* after an original by Veronese. On the right wall, *Louis XV in War* by Carl Van Loo; across from it, *Maria Leszczynska in Court Dress* wearing the crown jewels, also by Van Loo.

*The Salon de Mercure. Facing page: the Salon d'Apollon with the portrait of Louis XVI in coronation dress.*

**Salon de Mercure** - This room dedicated to Mercury was originally the king's room for lying in state. The imposing bed was placed facing the windows and set apart by a balustrade in solid silver that weighed a ton and that had been made by Alexis Loir et Villers, silversmiths from the Gobelins Manufactory. The balustrade was melted down together with numerous other gold and silver objects in December 1689 to bridge the deficit in the Treasury.

On the ceiling *Mercury on a Chariot Drawn by Roosters* by Jean Baptiste de Champaigne (1631-1681). In the coving *Alexander Receiving Ambassadors from India, Ptolemy with the Sages, Augustus Receiving Ambassadors from India* and *Alexander Turning Over Exotic Animals to Aristotle.*

On the walls, *Louis XV in his Coronation Dress.* Facing it, the queen *Maria Leszczynska.* Two other portraits of the monarchs are also in the room.

**Salon d'Apollon** - This room served as the Throne Room and the decoration was particularly important. Louis XIV's huge throne, in silver and 2.60 meters high, stood on a platform covered with a gold-ground Persian carpet. In the 18th century it was replaced by a throne in gilded wood, which no longer exists. Behind it was the tapestry with gold and silver threads now on the wall facing the window. One can still see the three hooks to which the canopy was attached. The ceiling was frescoed by Charles de Lafosse, with a representation of the *Chariot of the Sun*, an allusion to royal authority. In the vault arches, the *Four Parts of the World.* The six candleholders were made for the Hall of Mirrors, during Louis XV's reign.

But our attention is particularly drawn to the imposing presence of the king, present in the beautiful portrait painted by Rigaud in 1703. The king, 63 years old at the time, with a life full of marvelous achievements but also various vicissitudes behind him, is the very picture of majesty.

24

*View of the Salon de la Guerre.*

# SALON DE LA GUERRE

The Salon de la Guerre or Hall of War is at the back of the State Apartments at the corner of the northern and western facades. Construction was begun by Jules Hardouin-Mansart in 1678 and Le Brun finished the decoration in 1686.

The walls are covered with a facing of white and green marble up to the trabeation which acts as a cornice for the vaulting of the domed ceiling. The first thing we see upon entering is the enormous stucco medallion by Coysevox on one of the walls, representing Louis XIV dressed "à l'antique" with the fluent locks of his wig falling over his shoulder and with the staff of command in his right hand. The sovereign's horse tramples the fallen enemies. *Glory*, in the guise of a maiden leaning on an obelisk, symbolically raises her hand over the king's head. The two winged female figures

above the medallion represent Fame extolling the king, one with a trumpet, the other with a laurel wreath; below, two chained "prisons". The bas-relief that covers the fake fireplace represents Clio, muse of History, as she writes the feats of the monarch. This decorative complex extolling the glory of the king is particularly imposing.

The ceiling lunettes show the countries defeated by Louis XIV and Bellona, Goddess of War, against a stormy background. In the corners, the coat of arms of France among emblems of war.

In the central dome Le Brun has represented *Victorious France*. Particular attention should be paid to the finesse of the decoration consisting of cascades of arms and trophies, the doors and the simulated doors covered by mirrors framed in brass.

# THE HALL OF MIRRORS
## (GALERIE DES GLACES)

Louis XIV had it built in place of Le Vau's terrace which originally was a means of communication between the north and south pavilions. Work was begun in 1689 and lasted ten years.

The Gallery is 73 meters long, 10.50 meters wide and 12.30 meters high. The seventeen arched windows overlooking the garden are matched by the same number of simulated windows decorated with panel mirrors with beveled sides and framed in chased gilt brass. Four of these doors communicate with the King's apartments. Particular attention has been given to the decoration of this world-famous gallery. The spaces between the windows are scanned by engaged pilasters in red-brown marble of Rance with bases in chased gilded bronze and capitals invented expressly for this gallery by Caffieri. The frieze of the gilded stucco cornice is decorated with the emblems of the royal orders of Saint Michael and of the Holy Ghost. On the cornice are 24 groups of putti by the sculptor Coysevox and, everywhere, garlands, trophies and cascades of arms, by Coysevox, Tuby, Le Gros and Massou. In the time of the Sun King the furnishings in the gallery were of solid silver - the flower pots for the orange trees, the tables, the foot-stools, as well as the finest statues of the royal collections.

Access to this gallery, as well as to the whole apartment, was open to all and it swarmed with a motley crowd, from common people up to the grandest lords. Once it was even crossed daily by cows, asses and goats which were conducted to the apartments of Louis XV's daughters, who at the time were very small, so they could drink fresh milk every morning.

During the subsequent reigns, great receptions were organized for the arrival of various ambassadors, the visit of the Doge of Venice, princely weddings such as that of the duke of Burgundy in 1747 when a magnificent gala ball was held. On special occasions the king's throne was set up under a canopy at the back of the gallery, on the side of the Salon de la Paix.

Now the chandeliers in Bohemian crystal are still there to marvel at, the 24 torches from the time of Louis XV, the consoles in gilded wood with marble table tops, the porphyry vases, the antique busts... immersed in a fantastic world that transcends the man for whom it was made, Louis XIV, and the artists who worked there, a world to the glory and fame of all France.

*Overleaf: the Hall of Mirrors (Galerie des Glaces).*

*General view of the Hall of Mirrors (Galerie des Glaces).*

*Detail of the marble facing of the Hall of Mirrors.*

*On the opposite page: the Hall of Mirrors
with the gilded wood candelabra from the time
of Louis XV. Above: the Salon de la Paix.*

# SALON DE LA PAIX

Situated at the southwest corner, the Salon de la Paix or Salon of Peace, flooded with light, overlooks the parterres to the south with their marvelous flowered arabesques. The decoration is similar to that of the Salon de la Guerre, at the other end of the Gallery. Most of the decoration dates to the time of Louis XIV, except the large medallion above the fireplace which represents *Louis XV as Peacemaker*: the king is represented at the age of 19 in the act of handing an olive twig, symbol of peace, to Europe in the guise of a maiden. This work by Lemoyne, of 1729, is above the green marble fireplace. On the mantelpiece, two small busts of Roman emperors; in the hearth, a fine plaque with the coat of arms of France and Navarre and a pair of fine firedogs with two facing lions, specifically commissioned for this room from the sculptor Boizot by Marie Antoinette. On the marble walls, cascades of

arms and musical instruments. Attention should also be paid on the mirrored walls to the putti playing around vases of flowers as well as to the chandelier with the girandoles in amethyst-colored crystal.

The door is flanked on either side by a bust with the head in porphyry, set on a pedestal, as well as a vase of grey marble. Busts of this kind abound in the palace. A cornice resting on gilded wood brackets runs around the ceiling while in the corners the lyres and caducei mean that the arts and commerce prosper in peace. This room was separated from the Hall of Mirrors by a movable partition in the time of the queen Maria Leszczynska, which was at times removed for grand fetes. Depending on the occasion, it could be turned into a gaming room for the queen or a concert hall. On Sundays in winter the queen organized concerts of vocal and instrumental music which became famous. But,

*The ceiling of the Salon de la Paix.*

shy as she was, the queen made no effort to conceal her love for gambling, especially a game of chance called *cavagnole* at which she often lost.

The nobles who lived a spendthrift life in Versailles tried to recuperate their fortunes gambling. In all the periods there was always a "game room" in the apartments of the king, the queen and the members of the royal household. The games changed with the times but always represented a risk. Some lost their entire fortunes in the lapse of an evening, enriching their adversaries. Some of the ladies who played with the queen did not hesitate to cheat so they could buy a bauble they had their eyes on. The Princess d'Elbeuf, who had no resources of her own, even managed to live thanks to her winnings at the queen's table.

The domed ceiling was frescoed by Le Brun. At the center *France on a Chariot Drawn by Four Doves* surrounded by Peace, Glory and other peace-dispensing Virtues. In the semicircular compartments to be noted are Spain, Christian Europe Reconciled, Germany and Holland. The pendentives bear the arms of France and Navarre.

**Le Brun's Ceiling** - The ceiling celebrates the first 17 years of the reign of Louis XIV. Le Brun was assisted by his pupils in this colossal undertaking divided into 24 main compartments which are here listed beginning from the Salon de la Guerre: *The Alliance of Germany and Spain with Holland*, 1672; (right) *The Crossing of the Rhine in the Face of the Enemy*, 1672; (left) *The King Conquers Maastricht in 13 Days*, 1673; *The King Gives Orders to Attack the Major Dutch Garrisons Contemporaneously*, 1672; *The King Armed on Sea and Land*, 1672; *The King Governs Alone*, 1661; *The Pomp of the Powers near France*, 1674; *The Free County Conquered for the Second Time*, 1674; *The Decision to Declare War Against the Dutch*, 1671; *The Taking of Ghent in 6 Days*, 1678; *Ghent Defended by the Spaniards*; *Holland Accepts Peace Separating itself from Germany and Spain*, 1678.

Le Brun, who had left the mark of his genius in Versailles for a score of years during which he enjoyed the favor of the king, died forgotten. This is the fate that often befalls the greatest!

The Queen's Chamber (Chambre de la Reine).

# THE QUEEN'S APARTMENTS

**The Bedchamber** - Louis XV had the queen's chamber, originally done by Le Brun, redecorated in honor of his consort. The portrait of the king and that of her father, the unfortunate king of Poland Stanislas Leszczynski, were hung on the walls which were decorated with gold and flowers against a white ground. Yielding to all the desires of a queen who had given him several daughters and finally in 1729 an heir to the throne, the king provided a life of luxury for the queen, paying her gambling debts and renewing her household linens every three years from top to bottom, with sheets and bedspreads decorated with lace... at a cost of 30,000 French pounds, which was an enormous sum for those times! The room was always overflowing with a flurry of retinue. Once the duke of Luynes counted as many as 65 ladies in front of the railing which no one, except the king and queen, were permitted to pass. The queen could find some peace and quiet in the small drawing rooms behind the Grand Appartement, but they all disappeared in the renovation the next queen carried out.

When she became Queen of France, Marie Antoinette used this room, but she had to leave it almost as it was due to the insistencies of the architect Gabriel. The decoration by Robert de Cotte, Verberckt, Jules Dugoulon and Le Goupil was finished by Gabriel father and son.

In 1770 Antoine Rousseau added the Imperial Eagles of Austria to the royal coats of arms of France and of Navarre. The portraits of the mother of the queen, the empress Maria Theresa, her brother Joseph II and her husband Louis XVI were hung here in 1773. Subsequently the old mantelpiece was replaced by the one that is there now in mottled red and brown marble veined with white. Above it is a bust of the queen, by Lecomte, with the royal cloak and a medallion with the profile of Louis XVI.

The silk on the walls, in the furnishing of the alcove and the upholstering of the armchairs was changed with the seasons. The one there now is the "summer" model and was donated by the Lyon silk manufacturers. The design is particularly airy with interlacing flowers - roses, lilacs, tulips - tied with ribbons.

The domed ceiling is decorated with four trompe-l'œil paintings by Boucher. The overdoor decorations are by Natoire and Jean-François de Troy. Note should be taken of the fire screen by B.-Claude Séné (1748-1803), the foot-stools and the jewel-cabinet, of which more later.

At dawn on October 5, 1789, the mob which had arrived the day before from Paris invaded the palace. Monsieur de Miomandre, on guard, cried "Save the queen" and fell, as did Monsieur de Varicourt. Marie Antoinette had barely time to flee with the king through the small door at the right of the bed. She was never again to sleep here and died on the guillotine on October 16, 1793.

Nineteen "children of France" were born in public in this room where three queens, Maria Theresa, Maria Leszczynska, and Marie Antoinette, and two dauphines lived. According to an ancient custom, the queen was required to give birth to her children in public. It must be kept in mind that Versailles was open to all and was even more crowded when time for a birth drew near. On December 19, 1778, when Madame Royale came into the world, the room was filled by such a throng of curiosity seekers, with two young Savoyards even perched on the furniture to get a better vantage point, that the queen felt ill and the king himself opened the window to let in a bit of air.

*Below, left: detail of the silk wall covering in the queen's chamber; details are so finely reproduced that every single flower and even the eyes on the peacock feathers can be identified.*

*Right: the bed with a sumptuous bedspread; note the charming bouquet in the background.*

*On the opposite page: the bed, with its hangings and the canopy decorated with ostrich feathers and plumes.*

**The Large Jewel-Cabinet** - This incomparable piece of furniture, to be found in the queen's chamber, is well worth a closer look. It was made in 1787 by Jean Ferdinand Schwerdferger (1734-1818) cabinet maker of German origin.

With its sober yet rich lines, this fine cabinet anticipates the Empire style. It is enriched by inlays in mother-of-pearl and glass, plaques of blue and white Sèvres porcelain imitating Wedgewood, and with numerous bronze appliqués. The bronze caryatids represent the four seasons; the eight quiver-shaped feet are joined together, four by four, by cross-bars.

Facing page. Above, left: the Salon des Nobles.
Below: the Salon du Grand Couvert.

The Guard Room.

**The Salon des Nobles** - This room served the queen as *Grand Cabinet*. All that is left from the time of Maria Theresa is the ceiling by Michel Corneille. The rest of the decoration was done under Marie Antoinette by her favorite architect, Richard Mique (1728-1794), from 1785 on. The two chests of drawers (originally there were three) and the corner cupboards are by Riesener. Various important paintings include the portrait of Louis XV in his coronation dress by Cozette, woven on a Gobelins tapestry. The rock crystal chandelier is deemed to be one of the finest in Versailles and the floor is covered with a splendid Savonnerie carpet.

**The Salon du Grand Couvert** - When required this room did double duty as antechamber and as the queen's dining room. The table was set in front of the fireplace. On the ceiling *Dario's Family Prostrate at Alexander's Feet*, an old copy by Le Brun, replaces an original by Vignon which no longer exists. The vaults are decorated with paintings by Vignon. On the mantelpiece, *Sleeping Ariadne*, a copy by Pierre Julien (1731-1804) of the famous antique statue in the Vatican. The lovely paintings on the walls include the first *Portrait of Marie*

*Antoinette* (1779) in a marvelous carved frame and *Marie Antoinette with Her Children* by Vigée-Lebrun, as well as the portraits of the daughters of Louis XV - *Madame Adélaïde* and *Madame Victoire* - and, near the fireplace, *Madame Elisabeth in Spanish Dress*, by Adélaïde Labille-Guiard (1749-1803).

**The Guard Room** - It was originally the upper part of a chapel that was on the ground floor. In 1676, the old flooring of marble slabs was replaced by a wooden flooring in herringbone design. Le Brun made the fine facing of the walls in polychrome marble. The painted decoration was all done by Noël Coypel (1628-1707). At the center of the octagonal ceiling *Jupiter Crossing the Skies in His Chariot* is surrounded by numerous mythological figures. In the coving four subjects inspired by antiquity. In the corners the vivacious illusionistic representations create a perspective effect. The overdoor decorations in bas-relief by Le Gros and Massou bear the royal monogram and the fleur-de-lys. The Guard Room has the same type of geometric decoration as the *Queen's Staircase* which was a pendant to the Ambassadors' Staircase that led to the State Apartments. It was built in polychrome marble by Hardouin-

39

Mansart between 1679 and 1681. The imposing trompe-l'œil painting was done by Philippe Meusnier in 1701 who entrusted the execution of the flowers to Belin de Fontenay, painter at the Gobelins Manufactory, and a specialist in this decorative genre. The over-door decorations of the balcony and the group of cupids in gilded lead in the niche were made by Masson in 1681. This monumental staircase, an example of art under the reign of Louis XIV, leads to the Queen's Guard Room.

# SALLE DU SACRE

The Coronation Room was radically transformed by Louis Philippe so that two large canvases by David, the *Coronation*, which gives the room its name, and the *Distribution of the Eagles*, could be housed here. On the wall facing the windows a painting by Baron Gros: the *Battle of Aboukir*. On the ceiling, the *Allegory of 18 Brumaire* by Callet.

Louis David (1748-1825), a pupil of Vien, accompanied his master to Italy where he became acquainted with Roman antiquity. He became the founder of neoclassicism and returned to Rome where he painted the famous *Oath of the Horazii*. Politically committed, he had voted in favor of the death of the king and had become Superintendent of Fine Arts. Napoleon's epic gave him a chance to make use of his interests in antiquity, drawing a parallel between the ancient Roman emperors and the "small Corsican" covered with imperial eagles and devoured by ambition who had dragged his legions throughout Europe.

The *Distribution of the Eagles* was painted in 1810, the same year as the *Coronation* of which we have a copy here, made by the painter himself; the original is in the Louvre.

The coronation ceremony took on place December 2, 1804, in the cathedral of Notre-Dame in Paris. We know that the celebration was carried out in absolute adherence to the ceremonial dictates but that jealousy and grudges smoldered underneath. The emperor's sisters balked at having to carry Josephine's train; Letitia Bonaparte, Madame Mère, shown in the tribune, was not present at the ceremony, for she refused to watch the coronation of her daughter-in-law, whom she referred to as "this woman". The painting, with its 150 portraits, is an authentic page of history.

41

# THE GALLERY OF THE BATTLES

After the 6th of October, 1789, the palace gradually went into lethargy. Without its king, it was no more than a body without a soul. The Revolution had gone its way, heads had fallen. Louis Philippe put on the robes of the king of France. Versailles was too grand for the *citizen king*, who set up court at Trianon. The palace became a museum.

As work went on to change it into the Grand Museum, walls disappeared and so did fine marble mantelpieces in various rooms, splendid wainscotting was painted over until finally in 1837 the Gallery of the Battles was inaugurated in the south wing which had once contained the apartments of the *Enfants de France* and the royal family's close relatives.

The architects Fontaine and Nepveu built this vast gallery, 120 meters long, to house the paintings which commemorated the glories of the French armies from the first tribes gathered around Clovis up to the Grenadiers of Napoleon's Guard. But there was also an inherent political objective: the need to muster a large ensemble around the person of the *roi des Français*, satisfying those who were nostalgic for the *Ancien Régime* and at the same time rekindling the spirits of the Bonapartists with the ghostly beat of the marching boots of the Old Guard.

White busts, with immobile expressions, of questionable make, mark the stages of this history of France in pictures. But aside from the spirit, of a historian or an art lover, with which one proposes to visit the collection, an engraved plaque provides us with the true meaning of this gallery:

*"The busts in this gallery*
*are those of the princes of royal blood,*
*of the admirals, of the constables,*
*of the marshals of France*
*and of the famous warriors*
*who fell in battle for France".*

**Battle of Poitiers, October 25, 732** *(p. 44, above)* - Charles-Louis Steuben (1788-1856) was a famous French painter of German origin. A pupil of Gérard and official portrait painter, another aspect of his talent appears in this battle scene. The Saracens who had invaded almost the entire Mediterranean basin, from the Indus River to Spain, cross the Pyrhenees and invade Aquitaine, advancing as far as Poitiers. Charles Martel defeats them near the city and ousts them from the realm of the Franks. In this spacious composition Charles Martel appears in the center of the picture, on a white horse, brandishing the Frankish battle-ax in sign of victory.

**Wittekind submits to Charlemagne at Paderborn, in 785** *(p. 44 below)* - Defender of the Faith, Charlemagne is here shown as a peacemaker, in the act of inviting Wittekind and the peoples thronging behind him to receive the benediction from the hands of a priest. *Ary Scheffer*, born into a family of artists, was of Dutch origin. He had frequented the School of Fine Arts and had participated in the Salon of 1812, subsequently becoming one of the major exponents of Romanticism. Louis Philippe commissioned more than 30 episodes and portraits from him for the Museum.

**Count Eudes defends Paris from the Normans, in 886** *(p. 45, above)* - Victor Schnetz (1787-1870), a pupil of David and of Baron Gros, gives us another fine page of French history. Count Eudes, in the midst of battle, defends Paris from the Norman invaders. Despite his tenacious courage he was unable to completely oust these Scandinavian "men of the North". Crowded fortifications in flames act as background in the painting. Places like this and episodes like this already give a hint of the future importance of Paris.

**Battle of Bouvines, July 27, 1214** *(p. 45, below)* - With a theatric gesture Philippe Augustus places his crown on the altar giving his vassals the possibility of taking it and choosing the leader who would guide them to victory. The German emperor, the count of Flanders, and the king of England attempt to dismember France, which leads to the Battle of Bouvines and the muster around the Capetian crown. *Horace Vernet* describes a fascinating page of history with his precise brushstroke, rich color and unique light.

**Battle of Taillebourg, July 21, 1242** *(p. 46, above)* -
One can never render his just due to *Eugène Delacroix*
(1798-1863), one of the most fertile artists France ever
had. The vibrating colors, the precision of the details,
the vigor of the movement are all elements he has
masterfully used to represent the moment in which
Saint Louis, wielding his mace, pushes back the English
troops to the other bank of the Charente, on the bridge
of Taillebourg, forcing them to retreat.

**Battle of Marignan, September 14, 1515** *(p. 46, below)* - Marignan was not one of those battles that "saved
France". Even so in the hearts of Frenchmen it is synonymous with achievement and national prowess. It
was an act of inspiration, a gesture of glory and
audacity which induced the French to go over a pass
that had been held insuperable and rout the enemy.
The evening before the battle Francis I had his arma-
ture put on by Bayard, "Chevalier sans peur et sans

reproche". It was the beginning of a dream the king was
to pursue all his life: make Italy which shimmered
before him like a mirage his.
For *Alexandre-Evariste Fragonard* (1780-1850), son
and pupil of the *divin Frago*, and pupil of David,
painting concealed no secrets. He proudly presented
the king-knight on horseback the evening of the battle
while the peaceful proud gesture is full of promise.

**Taking of Calais, January 9, 1558** *(p. 47)* - The livid
light on the sea, the deserted ramparts... the battle is
won. François de Lorraine, Duc de Guise, did not
deign a glance at the dead, or at the dying youth in the
arms of his vanquished brother-in-arms. He will enter
through the breach and France will reconquer Calais
which England has so long contested.
*François Picot* (1786-1868) serenely sketches the event
with pleasing skillful brushstrokes, seductive and
banal.

**Entrance of Henry IV into Paris, March 22, 1594** *(p. 48)* - At two in the morning, in bad weather, some men clear away gabions which block the Porte Neuve. Charles de Cosse, Comte de Brissac, maréchal de France and governor of Paris, lets Henry IV into Paris, deceiving the papal legate, the duke of Feria, Philip II's ambassador at the League, and the commander of the Spanish garrison, Don Diego de Ibarre charged with safeguarding the interest of the Faith, that is of the Guise. In this picture we see him, hat in hand, leading the way for Bearnese who has put on his white scarf to confirm his dignity as Marshal. It is a joyous painting by *François Gérard*, Baron Gérard, the "painter of the king and the king of painters", in which the king's features, even though stereotyped are likeable.

**Battle of Rocroy, May 19, 1643** *(p. 49, above)* - The future "Grand Condé" seems particularly full of life and his horse also seems to be full of the same youthful ardor and aristocratic lineage. Armed men and musketeers move about excitedly around the victor of Rocroy who announces the victory enveloped in a halo of light and nascent glory.
The Spanish army which had been preparing to march on Paris has been dispersed and will not be able to rally.
*François-Joseph Heim* (1787-1865). Prix de Rome, has given us an outstanding demonstration of his talent.

**The Taking of York Town, October 17, 1781** *(p. 49, below)* - A decisive battle which ensured the Americans of their victory over the English during the War of Independence, where the efforts of the soldiers of the young United States and France were joined. *Auguste Couder* (1790-1873), who at the age of 77 published *Considérations sur le but moral des Beaux Arts*, has ably diffused a fine golden light on the banner in sign of victory.

**Battle of Fleurus, June 26, 1794** *(p. 50)* - In these years of the French Revolution, next to figures who were more or less fanatic, more or less corrupt, various military personalities emerged whom Napoleon picked for his own and who were to contribute to his glory.

The ever latent French genius is revealed in the great errors of history. For the first time these men who went to offer up their young lives on the battlefield realized that their blood sacrifice was a tribute to their *native land*. The Anglo-Dutch forces are defeated by Jourdan, his saber drawn, surrounded by Championet, Kléber, Marceau and a sad Saint-Just. In the sky, the painter *Jean-Baptiste Mauzaisse* has represented a hot air balloon which was used for the first time in this battle to spy the enemy's movements.

**Battle of Rivoli, January 14, 1797** *(p. 51, above)* - A limpid painting where the young general whose bearing is already regal is silhouetted against a background of snowcovered mountains.

"*...Et du premier consul déjà, par maint endroit,*
*Le front de l'empereur brisait le masque étroit.*" (Victor Hugo)

The artist who painted the young hero and presented his work at the Salon of 1845 was *Félix Philippoteaux* (1815-1884). The Austrians, commanded by Alvinczi, descend the slopes of Mount Baldo to confront the troops of Joubert, Masséna and Ney on the plain of Rivoli, and are overcome one after the other as they advance.

The wounded soldier who has fallen to earth casts a final glance, before dying, on the future of France.

**Battle of Austerlitz, December 2, 1805** *(p. 51, below)* - Austerlitz is the triumph of stratagy. On the anniversary of his coronation, Napoleon is victorious over the Austro-Russian coalition thanks to his skill in having suggested to the enemy the maneuvers which were to determine their defeat. *Gérard* (1770-1837) has succeeded in precisely rendering the confusion on the battlefield. In front of an expanse of the dead and the dying and broken arms, Rapp consigns General Repnin, who has been taken prisoner, to the emperor surrounded by his generals and companions in arms.

This Battle of Austerlitz, painted in 1810, was highly successful but apart from the undeniable skill of the artist it becomes obvious that his true vocation was portraiture.

**Battle of Iena, October 14, 1806** *(p. 52, above) - Horace Vernet* (1789-1863), who painted the last three pictures, was a Bonapartist and a good artist. Son, grandson and great grandson of painters, he was born with a brush in his hand and he knew how to use it in illustrating his period and above all the Emperor.

He had inherited an excellent luminist technique from his father, and in some of his paintings the figures are immersed in the light of the aurora borealis, as in the Battle of Friedland. In this Battle of Iena, Napoleon passes in review his troops and a soldier of the Imperial Guard, impatient, addresses him taking off his busby... Irritated, the emperor's attitude is such that we seem to hear the pawing of the shodden hoofs of his horse.

**Battle of Friedland, June 14, 1807** *(p. 52, below)* - Russia, which had come to the aid of Prussia after the defeat of Iena, was not defeated at Eylau and only

after the Battle of Friedland was Czar Alexander forced to sue for an armistice.

At the center of the picture, hat in hand, Oudinot receives Napoleon's orders. The soldier lying dead is a reminder that more than 40,000 died at Eylau and more than 30,000 died at Friedland and that more were to be added to this butchery.

**Battle of Wagram, July 6, 1809** *(p. 53)* - The picture was exhibited at the Salon in 1836. The emperor observes the advance of the Austrians. After the first day's fighting the outcome is still in the balance. The battle begins again at dawn. Davout, Masséna, Lassalle repulse the enemy attack. Just then Napoleon takes advantage of the confusion in the center of the Austrian ranks and launches an attack. The archduke Charles retreats and an armistice is requested on July 11th. This time 84,000 men have lost their lives in the field of battle.

# THE COUR DE MARBRE

The court of Louis XIII's château, which was surrounded on three sides by buildings, and which was later to become the Marble Court, was the nucleus of the palace.

From 1665 on Le Vau and then Hardouin-Mansart, in 1679, modified the original aspect, adding the 8 marble columns to the central body, the 84 white marble busts on corbels thas softening the austerity of the large windows in Louis XIII style with their small paned windows, and installing the balustrade on the roof and the dormer windows. The three windows on the first floor of the central body were only later provided with arches. They correspond to Louis XIV's chamber, ideally the center of the palace and the heart of France. The pediment is decorated with a clock flanked by Mars and Hercules, while the wings are surmounted by statues and flaming vases. Louis XIV must have considered the court to be a sort of sanctuary for he had it paved in marble and added steps so coaches could not enter.

On Luly 4, 1674, Quinault and Lulli had *Alcestes* given there for the celebrations in honor of Madame de Montespan. Another fete followed on July 28th, this time with a dinner, and a table was installed around a fountain in the midst of the court.

Marie Antoinette, who wanted to modernize the château, even thought of transforming it by closing the court with another wing in which case she would not have appeared on the balcony before the mob on October 8, 1789...

*The Salon de l'Œil-de-Bœuf.*

# THE KING'S APARTMENTS

**The Salon de l'Œil-de-Bœuf** - Courtiers waiting for the king to wake up - the *Lever du Roi* - waited every morning in this anteroom. Formerly the old chamber of the king and the Salon des Bassans were situated where the "Bull's Eye" room, which owes its name to the large oval opening in the vault, is now to be found. The frieze in the vault is decorated with gilded stuccoes of frolicking children on a hatched ground with rosettes. Various artists collaborated on the work: Corneille Van Clève who also did the high altar in the palace chapel, Simon Hurtelle (1648-1724), Anselme Flamen (1647-1717) a pupil of Marsy, Poulettier, Poirier and Hardy.

The walls are decorated with wainscotting decorated with garlands, tall mirrors which flood the room with light, and some fine portraits including *Louis XIV on Horseback* by Pierre Mignard (1612-1695), *Maria Theresa of Austria*, the king's wife, by Jean Nocret (1617-1672), who also painted the famous picture of *Louis XIV and His Family* here, where the figures are presented in the guise of gods.

This room served as an anteroom where the anxieties and hopes of the courtiers mingled with gossip and back biting and had very little furniture in it. At eight on the dot each morning the first valet would wake the king with the words "Sire, it is time" while the governess kissed his cheek. After a brief toilette attended to by the "blue valets" the door was opened and the persons of high rank came in for the "grandes entrées". Shortly thereafter the "secondes entrées" began after which the king dressed while his brother or a courtier kept him company. In the meanwhile in the Salon de l'Œil-de-Bœuf and in the Gallery everyone was waiting for the usher to announce "Gentlemen, the king" as he struck the floor once with the pole of his halberd. The right time to present the king with a petition or ask for a favor was as he was going to mass.

**The King's Chamber** - In the time of Louis XIII the room was used for receptions and overlooked the garden on one side and the Cour de Marbre on the other. When construction on the Hall of Mirrors began in 1679 the view over the gardens disappeared. In 1701 it became the King's chamber.

Great attention has been paid to the decoration with its white and gold. The tall grooved gilt piers are the only elements of the original decoration that have survived. The king's bed is behind a gilded wooden railing. The gold and silver brocade of the two armchairs, the back of the alcove, the curtains, the baldachin and the bedspread were expressly made by the textile manufactories of Lyons in 1980 after the original. Above the bed, on a hatched ground with rosettes, is a high relief by Nicolas Coustou, *France Watching Over the King's Sleep*. Originally there was only one fireplace in the room, the one on which the bust of Louis XIV by Coysevox is placed. Louis XV had the fireplace on the opposite wall built. The upper part of the mirror frame is a stylistic innovation. Five of the nine paintings by Valentin de Boulogne (1590-1632), a French painter of the school of Caravaggio, who worked in Rome, are inserted between the modillion frame and the ceiling. They represent the *Four Evangelists* and the *Tribute to Caesar*. There is also another painting, *Hagar in the Desert*, by Giovanni Lanfranco (1582-1647), a pupil of the Carracci.

Noteworthy the medallions above the doors, including a self-portrait by Van Dyck.

*Facing page: detail showing the rich textiles used for the king's bed, the doors and the furniture. The canopy of this bed, like the queen's, is surmounted by ostrich feathers and plumes.*

*Below: general view of the king's chamber. This is where the ceremony for the awakening of the sovereign took place, but Louis XV never slept in this room which was impossible to heat. He went there mornings and evenings in obeisance to the court etiquette and slept in a room in his private apartment.*

**The Council Hall** - This room communicates with the king's chamber and is illuminated by two windows and large mirrors. Reflected light and chandeliers were typical of the time. Louis XIV held his council meetings in this room which he took great pains to decorate with the finest pieces in his collections. He convoked his Secretaries of State here but also granted official audience to private individuals. Under Louis XV the Council Hall was enlarged by Gabriel, while the sculptor Jules Antoine Rousseau carved the marvelous wainscotting, decorated with various subjects and which is still there to be admired. The clock on the mantlepiece of the fine fireplace in mottled red and brown marble with a rich decoration in bronze is Louis XV but the two large vases, exquisite examples of the high level of refinement achieved by French porcelain manufacturers, were added by Louis XVI. One of the overdoor decorations is by Verdier, while the other three are by Houasse. The porphyry bust of Alexander the Great decorated with gilded bronze by Girardon was acquired by Louis XV expressly for this room, where up to the Revolution all the decisions of the realm were taken around the table which is covered with the same fabric as the walls.

*Facing page: bust of Louis XV by Coysevox, set on one of the two mantelpieces in the king's chamber.*

*Below: the Council Room with its rich tapestries.*

# THE QUEEN'S PRIVATE ROOMS

Louis XV had had these rooms installed for the queen behind her apartment. While the queen's apartment has a southern exposure and is flooded with light, these rooms behind overlook the Cour de Monseigneur, on the north. A wide balcony with a pergola and flowers was added to brighten the surroundings. When Marie Antoinette took over, she transformed everything for her personal use, heedless of expense. Richard Mique, her architect, was always busy satisfying the whims and caprices of his royal client in reorganizing the *Cabinet Doré*, the *Library*, and the *Bathroom*. All the rooms were filled with luxurious objects, in obeisance to the tastes of the queen.

Thanks to recent restoration, it once more looks as it did when Marie Antoinette left, with fine objects and furnishings which however did not belong to the queen, for hers were lost in the war.

**The Méridienne** - This exquisite little octagonal drawing room was expressly created by Mique for the queen's afternoon nap which was then known by the term "méridienne". The decoration is as refined as possible. The wainscotting was carved by the Rousseau brothers, painters and decorators, known for their ornamental motifs of Italian and specifically Pompeian inspiration.

In creating this small drawing room for the queen the artists outdid themselves in inventing sentimental attributes which the admiring gaze of the visitor can discover everywhere: garlands, wreaths of flowers, arrows, small animals and a thousand charming details typical of a period long past. Mirrored panels lined the back of the alcove that was upholstered with the same seeded light blue damask upholstery which covers the comfortable ottoman and the three small armchairs in gilded wood by Jacob.

The console in gilded wood decorated with a crowned dolphin celebrates the birth of the heir to the throne in 1781. The table in petrified wood with the base decorated with ram's heads and hoofs was given to Marie Antoinette by her sister Maria Anna of Hapsburg.

Before leaving the small drawing room, take a last look at the clock on the mantelpiece with the thought that time, here too, sometimes stopped for the charming queen born under a tragic star.

*Above: the Salon d'Or with a fine harp by Nadermann.*
*Below: detail of the neoclassic wainscotting (boiseries).*
*The perfume censer and the Greek sphinxes were typical 18th-century ornaments also used in the Empire style.*
*On the facing page: the Méridienne.*

# THE KING'S PRIVATE APARTMENTS

**Cabinet de la Pendule** - The carved and gilded wainscotting in this room is by Verberckt and the decoration is characteristic of late Louis XIV and early Louis XV. Over the doors, arcadian scenes painted by Boucher. The room takes its name from the astronomical clock invented by Claude Siméon Passemant (1702-1769), French clockmaker and optician, which was presented to the king in 1753 by the Académie des Sciences. The unusual mechanism made by Dauthiau is surmounted by a crystal globe with the moon and planets moving around the sun according to the Copernican theory. Jacques Caffiéri made the marvelous deoration in gilded bronze.

In the center of the room is a reduced version by Vassé of the equestrian statue of Louis XV. The original by Bouchardon was on what is now Place de la Concorde, formerly dedicated to Louis XV, and was demolished during the Revolution. At the sides of the room are two consoles in gilded wood with episodes from the royal hunting expeditions represented on the tops.

**Cabinet des Chiens** - The "room of the dogs" is the first anteroom in the king's private apartments. The decoration, inspired by drawings by Jules Hardouin-Mansart, was done in 1738.

Louis XV had the kennels of his pet dogs set up here. The stucco cornice is decorated with motifs of the hunt and animals while floral motifs appear in the large medallions.

*The Cabinet de la Pendule.*

*Facing page: the Cabinet des Chiens, and detail.*

The Salle a Manger des Retours du Chasse.

**Salle à manger des Retours de Chasse** - In 1750 this room began to be used as a dining room for the return from the hunt. The walls are clad with wainscotting which heralds Louis XVI style in its sobriety and elegance of line. On one side a *precision clock*, the works of which were made by Ferdinand Berthaud (1727-1807), a Swiss clockmaker who had settled in France and who was a specialist in precision mechanisms and nautical instruments, nominated by Louis XV inspector general of the machines of the Navy and court clockmaker.

The clock in this room is enclosed in a sumptuous case of ebony with a bronze group of *Apollo on His Chariot* on top.

When the king returned from the hunt, he would invite ladies and courtiers to dine here. The prerogatives of court ceremony were abolished and the guests sat where they pleased. If there were men only, the king invited two gentlemen to sit next to him. In his memoirs the Duc de Croÿ remembers one of these meals in which the king "had us sit next to him without the least distinction and we conversed with great familiarity, not forgetting however that we were in the presence of our king".

**The King's Private Study** - In 1753 Gabriel transformed an old billiard room where Louis XIV had installed some of his picture gallery into a private study for Louis XV. For the wainscotting the king turned once more to Verberckt who executed ten large panels carved with floral motifs and scenes of children, one of the artist's best works.

In 1739 the cabinetmaker Antoine Robert Gaudreaux offered the king a fine medal cabinet with magnificent decoration in bronze. Gilles Joubert added two corner cabinets made of violet wood with ormolu deco-

*Above: Louis XV's private study with the magnificent bureau à cylindre designed by Œben and finished by Riesener. Below: one of the corner cabinets made in 1755 by Joubert to match Antoine Gaudreaux's medal cabinet. The front is decorated with a medallion of three putti in the snow and medals which refer to the cabinet's use.*

ration in 1775.
However the most marvelous piece of furniture is the famous *bureau à cylindre for Louis XV*, considered one of the most beautiful desks in the world. It was commissioned from Jean-François Œben (1710-1763), a cabinet maker of German origin, who thanks to the protection of the Marquise de Pompadour was nominated *ébéniste du Roi* at the Gobelins Manufactory in 1754 and at the Arsenal two years later.
This desk is an authentic masterpiece not only of the art of intarsia and chasing but also in its mechanical perfection. In fact when the roll top was closed the drawers and the writing surface were completely blocked. Œben died before completing the desk and his pupil Riesener consigned it to the king in 1769. In 1794, at the height of the Revolution "all the attributes of feudalism", that is the king's initials, had to be removed.

**The New Rooms** - The three kings who lived in Versailles had so many changes made in the rooms, depending on what they needed them for at the time, that it is sometimes difficult to reconstruct the various phases of rearrangement. These rooms took the place of a small gallery which had in turn been obtained from part of Madame de Montespan's apartment. The new apartment was realized in 1752 for Madame Adélaïde, Louis XV's fourth daughter, who lived there until 1769.

The splendid wainscotting in the music room is carved with musical trophies.

When he was only eight years old Mozart played the harpsichord in this room for the king's family. The child prodigy fascinated the court of Versailles during his stay in Paris from November of 1763 to April of 1764. He lived with his father Leopold and his sister Maria-Ann in a house in what is now the rue François Miron.

In the past this palace, the hôtel de Beauvais, had belonged to Catherine Henriette Bellier, maid to Queen Anne of Austria and wife of Pierre de Beauvais, who was better known by her nickname of *Cateau la*

*Facing page: the Music Room, formerly Madame Adélaïde's private room. Above: detail of the decoration with a frieze and musical instruments.*
*Below: detail of Verberckt's magnificent boiseries.*

*Above: Louis XV's bathroom. The medallions represent scenes inspired by the pleasures of water.*
*Louis XVI transformed the room into a private study known as the Pièce de la Cassette.*

*borgnesse* (one-eye). The story is told of how, getting Louis XIV, who was then a youth of 16, off alone in a corner "she made a man of him in a few seconds..." King Louis XV did all he could to make these apartments more comfortable. The German-made majolica stoves he had installed could be removed in summer for esthetic reasons. He invented various devices to improve the draft in the chimneys of the fireplaces without much success, he improved the illumination of the staircases, and invented a fire fighting device. He also had sunshades installed at the windows which were then called "persanes" (jalousie) and it is thanks to him that Versailles had its first bathrooms and "English toilets".

Louis XV's bathroom is decorated with fine wood panels covered with gold in various colors. The medallions are carved with episodes that glorify the pleasures of water, framed by reeds tied with ribbons. One of the ovals shows a man who is teaching someone to swim. Louis XVI, who may not have found swimming so much to his liking, had this room used as an accessory to his study. It was known as Pièce de la Cassette and was where he kept his personal account ledgers.

**Louis XVI's Library** - In Madame Adélaïde's bedroom, which Louis XV had transformed into a gaming room, Louis XVI installed his personal library. Gabriel planned the decoration which was executed by Jules Antoine Rousseau (1710-1782), a French sculptor and decorator who also did the interiors of the Council Hall (1755) and the bathrooms (1770-1771). Louis Simon Boizot, a French sculptor who worked primarily with the Sèvres Manufactory, realized the marble decoration of the fireplace while the ornaments in bronze are by Pierre Philippe Thomire, who also worked at Sèvres. The medallions represent Apollo, the Arts, France with the portrait of the king...

This spacious room, characterized by sober decoration, contains fine pieces of period furniture: a commode by Benneman, of 1787, and, at the center, a round table in sequoia by Riesener. The chairs are by Séné (1784). The floor is covered by a large carpet. Louis XVI seems to have felt more at ease in this room lined with books, so much more intimate than the luxurious state apartments, and the king was often to the found here.

**The Porcelain Room** - The Marquise de Pompadour was the guiding spirit behind the fashion for fine French porcelain. Intelligent and gifted with exquisite taste, she managed to interest the king in the manufactories of Vincennes and Sèvres which produced such fine pieces that to promote sales the king consented to an exhibition of Sèvres porcelain in his private dining room. The courtiers had little choice but to buy.

**The King's Gaming Room** - After the *billiard room* is the *king's gaming room* (salon des jeux du roi), formerly the Cabinet of Marvels in Louis XIV's time and then anteroom in Madame Adélaïde's apartment. Despite the countless rearrangements this room, which has now been restored, is quite pleasing thanks to the furnishings which include a Savonnerie carpet, four corner cupboards with marquetry by Riesener and chairs by Boulard upholstered with a sumptuous silk from Lyon which harmonizes with that of the window drapes. On the walls, ten watercolors by Louis Nicolas Van Blarenberghe, painter for the Navy and the Department of War.

*Facing page. Above: Louis XVI's library.*
*Below: the Porcelain Room.*

*Below: Louis XVI's Gaming Room.*

*Bust of the Comtesse du Barry, by Augustin Pajou.*

*On the opposite page: the Apartment of the Comtesse in the palace.*

# THE APARTMENT OF THE COMTESSE DU BARRY

Originally the seven rooms on the second floor overlooking the Cour des Cerfs which go to make up the apartment that has taken its name from Louis XV's last mistress were occupied by members of the court. This extraordinarily beautiful woman, who cast a spell on Louis XV, was presented at court in the month of April 1769 and remained at Versailles for five years, until the death of the king. She had received an excellent education from the Dames de Sainte-Aure in Paris and had innate good taste. The apartment provided for her is characterized by a simplicity and essentiality of line, a style introduced by Madame de Pompadour and from which the Louis XVI style was to develop.

The wainscotting of the antechamber is covered with the famous Martin enamel. In their attempts to discover the secrets of Chinese lacquer, the four Martin brothers developed a type of resin-based paint which was quite successful. The technique was extremely painstaking for forty coats of paint had to be applied, each of which was carefully buffered. The translucency thus acquired made the panels and pieces of furniture glow like porcelain "in the manner of China and Japan". The antechamber also contains a graceful commode by Charles Topino (1730-1789) and a white majolica stove, like the one used in the time of the countess for heating.

In the library a bird cage decorated with porcelain flowers recalls the love for nature, sung by philosophers and writers of the time. A *corbeille* couch is upholstered with a costly textile of floral motifs. The bureau *à dos d'âne* is by Gaudreaux, first cabinetmaker to the crown, from 1726 to 1746. Note the chest of drawers by Riesener in the dining room and the so-called *mobilier de Choisy* in the large study comprising a series of chairs made by Foliot in 1770 for the château of Choisy-le-Roi.

Marie Antoinette was not fond of the king's mistress, perhaps because she feared she might lose her influence over her "cher papa" as she called Louis XV. In fact the evening of the king's funeral the new sovereign ordered Madame du Barry to withdraw to the abbey of Pont-aux-Dames. Let us leave the charming countess to her destiny which will lead her to the guillotine on December 8, 1793, almost two months after the queen.

Even though these rooms do not contain much furniture,
they give us an idea of the exquisite refinement of an epoch
in which ''sweet living'' was the fashion.
In the library, the bird cage with porcelain flowers and
the canapé à corbeille for tête-à-tête conversation.

Facing page: the finely decorated roof of the chapel
rises above the Italian-style balusters of the facade
of the North Wing overlooking the gardens.

# CORRIDORS, STAIRS, GALLERIES...

A countless number of passageways, hallways, stairs, corridors, galleries and mezzanines were created to keep the state apartments and the private apartments of the palace in touch. Nowadays despite the crowd of visitors which Versailles is never without, we find it hard to imagine as we pass through these halls and passageways that these carefully arranged spaces with their fine floors, enhanced by the presence of columns and sometimes of sculpture, were swarming with incredibly varied throngs of people.

Although the courtiers themselves seldom went to the ground floor, their footmen and sedan chairs did, adding to the confusion where the Swiss guards charged with keeping watch over the palace wandered around, on the lookout for some pretty wench in the throng of hucksters and pedlars to be found inside, outside, even in the most secluded passageways, selling everything. And nothing.

When construction work was going on, venders of food and drink were in demand to fulfill the needs of the masons, gilders, painters, carpenters, stone and wood carvers, who all mostly came from Paris.

And then there were merry soldiers from their barracks in the city searching for adventure, as well as the pages - young nobles assigned to duties in the king's apartments - who swelled the already conspicuous mass of idlers wandering through the corridors and loitering on the stairs.

In Louis XIV's time the Musique du Roi, or court orchestra, what with first and second violins, flutes, oboes, music masters and other masters, was formed of an incredible number of persons.

Generally it is believed that 10,000 people lived in Versailles - not counting the servants and the 30,000 skilled and unskilled workers when the important work was under way.

It takes little to imagine that it was a pick-pocket's paradise. Even King Louis XV had his watch stolen! Tired of ceremony, this shy, reserved king avoided the fetes and entertainments which had made his great grandfather, the Sun King, famous and preferred to withdraw to his private apartments or his beloved Petit Trianon.

The varied crowd has also disappeared and with it the stands and the shops, the enticing costermongers, and now we can pause to admire these spaces that were created for a world we can barely imagine in an atmosphere of an almost melancholy beauty.

# THE DAUPHIN'S APARTMENT

On March 30, 1349 the region called Dauphiné which stretches from the central area of the Alps up to the valley of the Rhône was assigned in appanage to the oldest son of the king of France. Actually, Humbert II (1333-1355), the king who at the time reigned over this region and who was without an heir and in deep waters financially, sold his possessions to the king of France after lengthy negotiations.

This eccentric figure later became a Dominican friar and the patriarch of Alexandria in Egypt. Dauphiné is indebted to him for the creation of important institutions such as parliament, the University of Grenoble and the State Audit court. Future King Charles V, son of John the Good, therefore became the first "Dauphin of France" in 1349. The last was the son of Charles X, Louis Antoine (1775-1844) who never mounted the throne.

The Dauphin Louis, son of Louis XV, first married Marie Therese Raphaëlle of Spain who died in 1746, and then Marie Josèphe of Saxony who was to give him seven children.

When he left the apartments of the Enfants de France, in the south wing, the young prince settled in the corner apartment on the ground floor, south side, of the central body. At the time of his first marriage the young bridal pair - he was 15 and she was 16 - went to live on the first floor of the south wing in a magnificent lodging that had expressly been redecorated. Two years later the princess died and the unconsolable Dauphin received his new bride in the same apartment, slightly changed, until the apartment on the ground floor where he had lived in his youth had been redecorated.

The apartment consisted of a first anteroom, a second anteroom under the Hall of Mirrors with two windows on the Parterre d'eau. This was followed by the chamber and the corner salon, beautifully lighted by four windows, two on the Parterre d'eau and two on the south parterre. The last rooms were the library with small adjacent rooms, and the bedchamber.

Most of the rooms in this charming apartment, like so many others, were destroyed in the course of time.

*Ground floor, the Dauphin's Apartment.*

*Facing page: the fireplace in the apartment.*

*The Dauphin's Chamber. Above: general view. Below: a fine piece of furniture in Chinese lacquer. Facing page: the library.*

Early in the 20th century, Pierre de Nolhac, historian and curator of the palace, restored them.

It is rather difficult to imagine these apartments without their woodwork and original furnishings. An attempt has therefore been made to recreate a certain harmony and a certain reflection of what they were or represented in the Dauphin's time.

The Chamber still contains all of Verberckt's (1704-1771) wainscotting. The fireplace of brownish red variegated marble is decorated with bronzes by Caffieri (1678-1775) representing *Flora* and *Zephyr*.

The overdoor decorations were painted in 1748 by Jean-Baptiste Pierre (1714-1789), a pupil of Natoire and last exponent of the rococo style.

The lovely portraits of the prince's sisters, Madame Adélaïde as *Diana* and Madame Henriette as *Flora*, painted by Nattier in 1742, can also be admired.

In the Grand Cabinet, paintings by Jean Baptiste Oudry (1686-1755) have replaced Nattier's overdoor decorations which represented the sisters the Dauphin was so fond of. There are exquisite paintings which are a joy to behold for by a skillful use of color the artist has infused his figures with infinite grace.

The large flat writing table, very elegant with its fine

*The Dauphine's Apartment. Above: general view. Below: detail of the* boiseries *beautifully lacquered in green.*

wrought bronze, was made by Bernard Van Riesen Burgh around 1745 for the Grand Cabinet. He was one of the three cabinet-makers of Dutch origin of the same family and with the same name who signed their furniture, which was typical of French 18th-century taste, with the imprint B.V.R.B.

The library has overdoor decoration by Vernet and a fine chest of drawers lacquered in vernis Martin, by Gilles Joubert (1689-1775).

The Dauphin had only to cross a corridor, whether from his library or from the corner drawing room, to reach his wife's room. Notwithstanding, the first antechamber is situated at the other end of the four-room apartment.

In the first antechamber is a portrait of the six-year old Louis XV, by Rigaud, in coronation dress ornamented with ermine and the fleur-de-lys. In the second antechamber is a painting of Louis XV by Van Loo. The original decoration, here and in the adjacent Grand Cabinet, of wainscotting by Verberckt has disappeared. The wood panelling of the chamber was executed in the workshop of Verberckt. The last three kings of France - Louis XVI in 1754, Louis XVIII in 1755, and Charles X in 1757 - were born here.

# MARIE ANTOINETTE'S
# GROUND FLOOR APARTMENT

Formerly the apartment of Madame Sophie and Madame Louise, these rooms are under the Salon de l'Œil-de-Bœuf, the king's chamber and the Council Hall and lead directly to the Cour de Marbre. Marie Antoinette installed her Petit Appartement there on the ground floor: a small salon, a chamber, a central vestibule and a bath.

The queen, who has been studied by various scholars, apparently followed her personal whims and the suggestions of a very limited circle of friends. But without trying to excuse or blame her, it might be opportune to remember that she arrived in France, fawned on, at the age of fifteen and that she was only nineteen when she became the queen of a lovely flourishing country, the most powerful in Christendom. At that age a person can still be easily influenced.

One caprice followed another and in 1782 at the death of Madame Sophie she decided to take this tiny apartment for herself. It should really be called a *pied-à-terre* since it was on a level with the Marble Court. Everything was green. Green damask for the bed, for the doors, the wardrobes in the library inherited from Madame Sophie. Shortly thereafter the original window was replaced by a French window on the Marble Court. In 1785, on the eve of the Revolution, she decided to have Madame Sophie's old library torn down. Her orders were immediately put into effect. Mirrors were to be installed in place of the library so as to provide the room with greater luminosity and at the same time create an indirect illumination.

Jean-François Heurtier (1739-1822) received the orders of the queen regarding the library... and the counter order as soon as the work was begun.

But these works on the small apartment on the Marble Court were the last the unfortunate queen was to order...

*Marie Antoinette's chamber in the queen's ground-floor apartment overlooking the Marble Court.*

*Above: the Grand Salon of Madame Victoire.*

*On the opposite page. Above: large corner room. Below the Salon des Nobles.*

# THE ROOMS OF THE DAUGHTERS OF FRANCE

Louis XV had ten children by his wife Maria Leszczynska, eight of which were girls. Living quarters for all these persons, including the servants and the small retinue that had grown up around the numerous family, had to be found. The first three daughters (Louise Elisabeth, Henriette and Adélaïde) remained in Versailles while the four younger daughters were sent to the Abbey of Fontevrault to receive an education. One of them, Madame Sixième, died there in 1744 at the age of eight. In 1793 Louise-Elisabeth married an Infant of Spain and left the castle where her two sisters, Madame Henriette and Madame Adélaïde, remained. After having spent their childhood in the apartments known as those of the Enfants de France situated in the south wing, they settled in the Dauphin's apartment on the ground floor, in the central part of the palace, facing the south parterre (Parterre du Midi) where the king, who was very attached to his family, paid them visits.

In 1748 Madame Victoire returned from Fontevrault to be followed two years later by her sisters Sophie and Louise. Henriette died in 1752 and Madame Adélaïde moved from their apartment to some rooms adjacent to the parterre on the north.

After various moves, Louis XV's daughters gradually settled down in the central part of the ground floor where Louis XIV's old Appartement des Bains had been. Their apartments extended as far as the king's Small Court (Petite Cour du Roi) which was then called Cour de Mesdames, and as far as the Cour aux Cerfs, partially transformed into a garden with fountains and rocaille decoration.

At present the apartments of Madame Victoire and Madame Adélaïde have been carefully restored to bring them back to what they were before they were remodelled in Louis Philippe's time. Unfortunately the original furniture was lost during the Revolution.

In 1768 Louis XV wanted to offer his new mistress,

Madame du Barry, a lovely apartment and asked his oldest daughter to give up hers on the first floor. Adélaïde then joined her sisters on the ground floor and being the oldest chose the best apartment, rather upsetting Madame Victoire who already lived there. A considerable amount of remodeling was needed so as to lodge the princesses Sophie and Louise "as their rank required". The Lower Gallery was used for this. These continuous changes, remodeling, transformation which must have required enormous sums of money now surprise us. At the time, Madame Adélaïde had two antechambers, a large drawing room, a bed chamber, an internal salon and a library. Now various mementos of this daughter of Louis XV, including a fine organ, are kept here.

**Staircase of Louis Philippe**, from the period of Louis Philippe, is an extremely modest structure despite the fact that its name evokes broad steps with banisters full of trophies of arms and imposing flights of stairs. It replaces Louis XIV's Ambassadors' Staircase which was the outstanding architectural masterpiece of the palace. This staircase was built to plans by Mansart and Charles Le Brun between 1674 and 1678. It was all of polychrome marble and consisted of eleven stairs in red marble with beveled corners which led up to a

*Madame Adélaïde's apartment. Above: chest of drawers in ebony and gilded bronze in the chamber. Below: Library or private study with a* bergère *bearing the mark of Pothier, and the organ that belonged to Madame Adélaïde.*

central landing decorated with a splendid fountain whose basin was also of red marble supported by two gilt bronze dolphins. The fountain was topped by a sculptural group that was a gift from a prince of the Albani family. Two flights of 21 stairs each led to the first floor to doors, carved by Caffieri, which opened onto the Rooms of Diana and Venus. A skylight let in light. The vaults were decorated with lovely paintings by Le Brun while the walls of the first floor, scanned by engaged pilasters in red marble with gilt bronze capitals, were covered with frescoes by Van Meulen representing the Four Parts of the World. In 1750 Louis XV had this magnificent architectural ensemble taken apart piece by piece and the rather commonplace staircase which took its place cannot but increase our regret at having lost so much.

The room known as *Hoquetons* was originally the Guard Room of the palace gendarmerie (Prévôté de l'Hôtel). The name derives from the tunic, called *hoqueton*, the palace guards wore. Their job was to keep order and it is not hard to imagine that they must have had their hands full trying to keep the confusion in Versailles under control. As a result they enjoyed great prestige. They wore bright red, blue and white tunics and carried cudgels which could be used in breaking up a riot or discouraging malefactors.

*The staircase Louis Philippe.*

*The Room known as* Hoquetons.

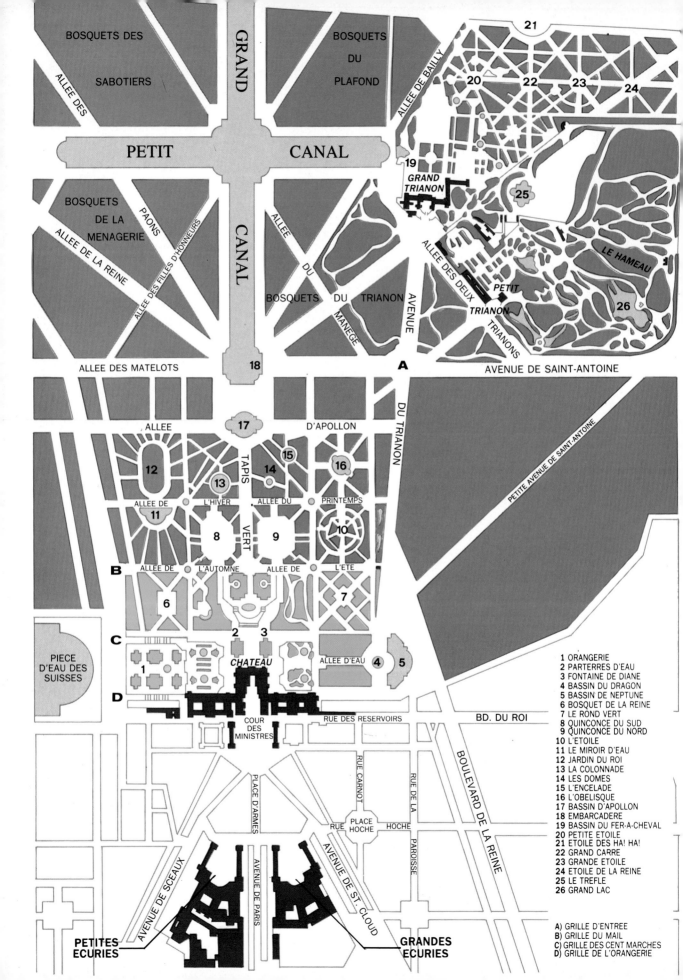

BOSQUETS DES SABOTIERS

ALLEE DES

GRAND

PETIT CANAL

CANAL

BOSQUETS DU PLAFOND

ALLEE DE BAILLY

21

20    22    23    24

19

GRAND TRIANON

25

LE HAMEAU

BOSQUETS DE LA MENAGERIE

PAONS

ALLEE DE LA REINE

ALLEE DES FILLES D'HONNEURS

ALLEE DU

ALLEE DES DEUX

PETIT TRIANON

26

BOSQUETS DU TRIANON

AVENUE

MANEGE

TRIANONS

ALLEE DES MATELOTS

18

A

AVENUE DE SAINT-ANTOINE

DU TRIANON

ALLEE

D'APOLLON

17

PETITE AVENUE DE SAINT-ANTOINE

12

TAPIS

15

16

14

13

L'HIVER    ALLEE DU    PRINTEMPS

ALLEE DE

11

VERT

8    9    10

B    ALLEE DE    L'AUTOMNE    ALLEE DE    L'ETE

6    7

C    2    3

CHATEAU

1    ALLEE D'EAU    4    5

PIECE D'EAU DES SUISSES

D

COUR DES MINISTRES    RUE DES RESERVOIRS    BD. DU ROI

PLACE D'ARMES

RUE CARNOT

RUE DE LA

BOULEVARD DE LA REINE

RUE    PLACE HOCHE    HOCHE

RUE PAROISSE

AVENUE DE SCEAUX

AVENUE DE PARIS

AVENUE DE ST. CLOUD

PETITES ECURIES

GRANDES ECURIES

1 ORANGERIE
2 PARTERRES D'EAU
3 FONTAINE DE DIANE
4 BASSIN DU DRAGON
5 BASSIN DE NEPTUNE
6 BOSQUET DE LA REINE
7 LE ROND VERT
8 QUINCONCE DU SUD
9 QUINCONCE DU NORD
10 L'ETOILE
11 LE MIROIR D'EAU
12 JARDIN DU ROI
13 LA COLONNADE
14 LES DOMES
15 L'ENCELADE
16 L'OBELISQUE
17 BASSIN D'APOLLON
18 EMBARCADERE
19 BASSIN DU FER-A-CHEVAL
20 PETITE ETOILE
21 ETOILE DES HA! HA!
22 GRAND CARRE
23 GRANDE ETOILE
24 ETOILE DE LA REINE
25 LE TREFLE
26 GRAND LAC

A) GRILLE D'ENTREE
B) GRILLE DU MAIL
C) GRILLE DES CENT MARCHES
D) GRILLE DE L'ORANGERIE

# THE GARDEN

Even as work on the château was in progress, Louis XIV turned to the gardens. He entrusted the plans to Le Nôtre whose genius he had enviously admired in the gardens of Vaux-le-Vicomte.

To judge from the interest he showed in the plans it seems likely that the park fascinated the king more than the castle.

Le Nôtre was a god as far as gardens were concerned and his was the secret of the art of perspective. He invented, created, recreated, Nature; he strewed maples and beeches and elms over the grounds, modelled the hawthorne, planted the linden tree, planned a grove, created a labyrinth and fascinated the king with his creative fantasy.

Fouquet, the superintendent of finances who had fallen into disgrace, was in prison. In 1665 his property was put on auction in order to pay his debts and the king jumped at the chance to get hold of the objects that had aroused his envy during the famous fete of August 17, 1661, which had been fatal for the ambitious superintendent. In addition the king had various kinds of trees removed from the estate of Vaux and numbers of orange trees found their way to Versailles.

In 1683, Fouquet's son, short on money, sold the king the herms in white marble which now embellish the Quinconces to the north and south. Later seventy chestnut trees from the park of Vaux were transplanted to the gardens of Trianon.

In 1664 the gardens of Versailles served as setting for a memorable fete in honor of Mademoiselle de la Vallière which was to pass into history: the Plaisirs de l'Île enchantée. With ballets, illumination, comedies and music, the fete was directed by two illustrious figures, Molière and Lulli. Equally famous fetes were organized in 1668, 1674, 1689 and in 1699...

This was what the king intended the garden to be used for - fetes as well as promenades. In the course of the numerous revisions, the cave of Thetis, which La Fontaine cites with his incomparable style in the Loves of Psyche, and other things as well, disappeared.

The problem of supplying water for the 1,400 fountains and pools also had to be solved. These gardens cover an area of 100 hectares, and they extend from the castle to the Etoile Royale for a total of three kilometres while the Grand Canal by itself measures 1.6 kilometers. There are so many statues and groups of figures in bronze and marble that count has been lost. As in Charles Trenet's famous song, it can truly be said: "It's an extraordinary garden".

Facing page. Above: a group of putti in the parterres d'eau in front of the facade overlooking the gardens. Below: parterre d'eau, statue representing the Loire.

Above: flower "embroideries" in the flower beds.

**The Parterre du Midi and the Orangerie** - The delicately embroidered flowerbeds have always roused great admiration. Two odd sculptures greet us as we approach - two marble sphinxes sculptured by Louis Lerambert (1620-1670 with bronze cupids, by Jacques Sarrazin, climbing over them. Not far away are some bronze vases by Ballin and the statue of the *Sleeping Ariadne* who seems to be dreaming of Theseus, a work by Van Clève.

On either side of the parterres the eye roams freely over the Orangerie, the Swiss lake and, in the distance, the wood of Satory.

The Orangerie was built by Hardouin-Mansart in two years, beginning in 1684, to protect the oranges and oleanders in the cold season. Around a large round basin, six grassy lawns are defined by double hedges of box between which are planted multicolored flowers.

A better idea of the imposing construction can be had by descending one of the two flights of a hundred stairs (*Escaliers des Cent Marches*). Piers decorated with statues and fine railings stand at the bottom of the stairs. Further on, the Pool of the Swiss owes its name to the regiment of Swiss guards who did the excavation. Although originally the lake was slightly smaller than it is now, the task took on colossal proportions. The present body of water is 282 meters long and 234 meters wide. The material from the excavation was used to fill in a pond then turned into the king's vegetable garden.

At the end was Bernini's statue of Louis XIV. The king had it set up in this secluded spot because as far as he was concerned the figure bore no resemblance to him and seemed to be riding an uncouth draft horse rather than an elegant steed.

*The Orangerie from the hills of Satory in a painting of the 18th century.*

*Facing page. Above: the Orangerie as it is today. Below: the Swiss pool.*

*Jets of water rain down on the group of Latona and her Children set on a rock in the fountain.*

**Bassin de Latone** - This pool already existed at the time of Louis XIII's hunting lodge but it was not until 1670 that the elegant group sculpture of *Latona and her Children* by Balthasar Marsy was set up on a rock. The story of the mythical Latona is anything but dull. Daughter of a Titan, loved by Jupiter, she gave birth to two children, Apollo and Diana, in the shade of an olive tree. One day while she was resting in the land of Caryae she asked some peasants for a drink of water to quench her thirst. When they derided her she asked Jupiter to avenge the insult and he transformed the insolent peasants into frogs.

In 1689 the fountain was reorganized by Hardouin Mansart and the sculpture which faced the castle was turned towards the lawn and the Grand Canal. The various level of the fountain are decorated with frogs, turtles and figures, in lead coated with bronze, while more than 50 jets of water animate the composition. To the left and to the right, in the flower beds, are the two *Lizard fountains* by the Marsy brothers. The fine marble vases are copies of originals from Italy and elsewhere. Those that represent the infancy of Mars were designed by Hardouin-Mansart.

On the right, note should be taken of the *Nymph with a Shell*, copy of an original by Coysevox to be found in the Museum of the Louvre. Right opposite is an equally famous work, the *Dying Gladiator*, copied by Mosnier from an antique original.

**The Colonnade** - The Colonnade was realized by Hardouin-Mansart between 1685 and 1688. Louis XIV was rather puzzled by this impressive piece of architecture which had been intended simply as decoration for a corner of the park and asked Le Nôtre's opinion. The architect answered: "Sire, your Majesty has made a gardener of a mason and he has served you making use of his trade".

Despite the perplexity of the king and of Le Nôtre, the fine colonnade in polychrome marble is quite striking. Thirty-two columns with Ionic capitals and the same number of piers behind form a circle 32 meters in diameter. Each arcade between the columns contains a marble basin with a jet of water.

At the center was the *Rape of Proserpine* by François Girardon (1627-1715). He was a highly gifted sculptor and completed his studies in Rome before becoming one of Le Brun's best collaborators. Quite a few of his works are to be found in the gardens of Versailles such as, for example, the statue of *Winter* in the northern parterre, the *Fountain of Saturn*, the *Bath of the Nymphs*, and, in particular, *Apollo attended by the Nymphs*.

Depending on the occasion, the colonnade was used for lunches, dinners and concerts.

*Statues in the woods of the Three Fountains.*

*The Colonnade.*

*The Bassin d'Apollon and the Grand Canal in a painting
by Pierre-Denis Martin (ca. 1663-1742).*

**Bassin d'Apollon** - In 1661 Louis XIV firmly established his personal power, appealing to "divine right" and choosing the sun as his emblem. This is why he must have been singularly delighted in seeing Apollo, son of Jupiter and Latona, God of Light, of the Arts and Letters, the most handsome and noble of the gods of Olympus, drive the chariot of the sun: the *Sun King*, in other words.

This extraordinary sculpture in gilded bronze was executed by Jean Baptiste Tuby (1635-1700) on a design by Le Brun. It dominates the center of a pool that has a maximum diameter of 110 meters. Apollo on a chariot drawn by four fiery steeds rises from the water surrounded by Tritons who blow their conch shells to announce the rising of the sun.

The fountain is particularly impressive in the days of the so-called *Grandes eaux*, when all the jets are in function.

The Grand Canal stretches out behind Apollo's fountain. Excavated at the time of Louis XIV, it took a dozen years to complete. This magnificent lake covering an area of 23 hectares, was in the past animated by numerous entertainments and when the Serenissima sent some gondolas for a fete in 1687, a corner of Venice was unexpectedly recreated here. Nowadays boats can be hired and it is without doubt an ideal place to practice rowing.

Near Apollo's fountain, on the right, is the *Fountain of Enceladus*, which represents the giant overwhelmed by the rocks on which he had dared to try to climb to Olympus. The composition is particularly effective and impressive, with the hand of the giant who tries in vain to get a hold on the stones as he sinks into the water, and with the powerful jet of water shooting out of his mouth to a height of 23 meters.

In the adjacent grove, the *Obelisk* is composed of 230 jets of water, 25 meters high at the summit.

A stroll will bring us to the *Fountain of Flora*, representing *Spring*, by the hand of Tuby, showing the goddess reclining among flowers and surrounded by frolicking cupids. The octagonal *Basin of Ceres* is decorated with a sculpture by Regnaudin: the goddess reclines on the harvest and with upraised eyes seems to be offering the riches of the earth to heaven.

*Apollo on his chariot rising out of the water surrounded by tritons and dolphins.*

**The Terrace and the Parterre du Nord** - The central body of the facade rises up on a terrace overlooking the gardens with a magnificent view of Le Nôtre's masterpiece.

Two imposing marble vases, the *Vase of Peace* by Tuby and its pendant, the *Vase of War* by Coysevox, are set respectively in correspondence to the windows of the Salon de la Paix and the Salon de la Guerre, to define the space of the terrace.

Down a few steps which lead to the gardens, are two vast parterres d'eau, large basins with their borders ornamented with exquisite sculptures commissioned by Colbert and realized on designs of Le Brun.

In front of the north wing are the fabulous plots designed by Le Nôtre, no longer flower embroidery as it was in front of the south wing, but with rows of box-trees which enclose flowered arabesques. To be noted, as in the southern parterre, the vases by Ballin and a shy *Kneeling Venus* by Coysevox. Oblivious to such reserve the sirens of the *Fountain of the Crowns* (*Bassin de Couronnes*) by Le Hongre and Tuby joyously splash in the company of tritons.

At the back of the parterres is the *Fountain of the Pyramid* by Giraudon after a design by Le Brun. This fountain, with water that cascades from the urn at the top into the four superposed circular tubs, is decorated with lead sculptures representing tritons, dolphins and crawfish. The young tritons in the first tub are particularly lovable and seem to effortlessly sustain the weight of the dolphins in the upper basin.

A fine view of the fountains of Ceres and of Flora can be had from here...

*Below: the gardens of Versailles seen from the side of the Parterre du Nord in a painting by Etienne Allegrain (1653-1736). In the lower part, Louis XIV with his courtiers.*

*Facing page. Above: the facade seen from the Parterre du Nord. Below: the Fountain of the Pyramid.*

One of the 22 basins in the Allée des Marmousets.

Glory with a medal bearing the effigy of Louis XIV
with Envy at her feet.
Facing page: the Bassin de Neptune.

**Bassin de Neptune** - Louis XIV had once said "I want children everywhere". As we walk through the park we become aware that his orders were scrupulously carried out for the compositions of mythological figures and the decorations of the vases are often gladdened by laughing impish putti and cupids. An example is the charming avenue called *Allée des Marmousets*, "marmousets" meaning urchins. The fantasy of Claude Perrault envisioned a decoration consisting of twenty-two circular basins of white marble with groups of three children in bronze at their center supporting basins of pink marble from Languedoc.

Various sculptors worked on these charming masterpieces, including Le Gros, Le Hongre, Lerambert, Mazaline and Buirette, which explains the diversity of style in the figures. The three infant satyrs by Le Gros are the very picture of gracefulness with their chubby hands, carefully arranged curls and hairy hoofs. Equally charming are the music-making putti by Lerambert and the two cupids with a little girl by Le Hongre. This is by far one of the most enchanting avenues in Versailles.

Our small urchins seem to have no fear of the *dragon* nearby who dominates the circular fountain, further down, surrounded by cupids riding swans and threatening the dragon with their darts. Further back is the *Fountain of Neptune* on which Le Nôtre, Hardouin-Mansart and Le Brun collaborated between 1679 and 1684. It was rearranged by Gabriel who added the imposing groups of sculpture which include *Neptune and Amphitrite*, by Sigisbert Adam, and the *God Ocean* on a marine monster, by Lemoyne. On the days of the *Display of Fountains (Grandes Eaux)* the fountain offers one of the most extraordinary sights in the garden.

# THE GRAND TRIANON

In the back of the park, hidden by majestic tall trees, is the Grand Trianon whose name derives from the village and adjacent lands which Louis XIV acquired so as to enlarge his possessions. In 1670 Louis XIV requested Le Vau to build him a pavilion which was called Porcelain Trianon since it was externally faced with blue and white majolica tiles from Delft, Nevers, Rouen and Lisieux. But the pavilion was not built to withstand time and weather and the maintenance costs for such a small structure seemed excessive to the Sun King who was used to things done on a grand scale. It was decided to replace the building with a pavilion in marble and the works were commissioned from Hardouin-Mansart in 1687. Robert de Cotte also had a hand in the plans and built the peristyle which served the king as dining room during the summer. Little by little the building was enlarged. It consisted of one floor crowned by an Italian-style balustrade, with the facade decorated with pilasters in pink marble from Languedoc and with Ionic capitals.

Jussieu and Richard planted a botanic garden at the time of Louis XV and subsequently a farm was installed on the surrounding land. But the king rarely visited the Grand Trianon where Czar Peter the Great and the king's in-laws stayed for a while. Shortly thereafter the Petit Trianon was built and the preceding building was neglected. King Louis XVI showed no interest in it and not until Napoleon did the Grand Tria-non once more come into its own. Restoration was begun in 1805. In 1810 the emperor often went there with his consort, Marie Louise, who was particularly fond of it. Louis Philippe then entrusted the architect Charles Nepveu (1777-1860) with more restoration; subsequently the queen, Marie Amélie, lived there with the sister of Louis Philippe, Madame Adélaïde. In 1845 the queen of Belgium, who was Louis Philippe's daughter, and her husband were guests there.

In the years between 1963 and 1966 Général De Gaulle decided to have this dwelling radically restored. It now serves as residence for heads of state on official visit and is sometimes used for the receptions of the president of the Republic.

*Series of rooms leading to the boudoir.*
*Below, left: the Boudoir.*

**The Boudoir** - The first three entrance rooms, containing a bust of Napoleon, various paintings by Houasse from other rooms in the building, and some views of the castle by Denis Martin, lead to a gallery that is decorated with a series of prints showing Louis XIV's military campaigns. A corner room at the end is the *Boudoir* of Empress Marie Louise. The "triumphal arch" desk in mahogany with bronze fittings belonged to the empress Josephine, Napoleon's first wife. It came here in 1809 after their divorce. The chairs were commissioned by Pauline Bonaparte. The room has an air of quiet and serene comfort.

The apartment reserved for foreign heads of state begins on the left and is not open to the public. To the right are the historic state apartments.

*The Room of Mirrors (Salon des Glaces).*

**The Room of Mirrors (Salon des Glaces)** - This corner room is particularly luminous thanks to the tall windows and the mirrors which give it its name. The frieze with children bearing symbols of war and peace are indicative of Louis XIV's influence and he used it as a Council Chamber. It then also served the Grand Dauphin in 1703. Louis XV made a few modifications and Louis XVI once more made it his Council Chamber. Napoleon's mother had the Grand Cabinet meet here, as did Empress Marie Louise, after which, in 1830, in the time of Louis Philippe the Council Chamber was reinstated. The light blue silk damask of the windows and the mirrors was chosen for Compiègne by Marie Antoinette but she never saw them, for they were not installed until Napoleon's time, together with the two fine mahogany consoles with bronze fittings and the small round tables (*guéridons*) by Jacob-Desmalter. The *athénienne*, an antique type of tripod table, has a circular top made out of a tombstone. The tables and the piano were made for Marie Louise in 1810.

**The Bedchamber** - The room had served as bedroom for Louis XIV and then for his son, the Grand Dauphin, in 1705, before being remodelled for the empress Marie Louise. In 1805 the dividing wall that existed in Louis XIV's time and had later been torn down was rebuilt in correspondence to the columns. In 1950 it was once more eliminated.

The balustrade of the alcove was made in 1810 by Marcion, a famous cabinetmaker (*ébéniste*) who was one of the group of artists engaged for the Garde-Meuble, the storage room for the court furnishings. The double-faced console is the work of another famous *ébéniste*, Jacob-Desmalter. The set of tea cups in Sèvres porcelain belonged to Marie Louise. The bed now there was commissioned by Napoleon for the palace of the Tuileries and is the bed in which Louis XVIII drew his last breath in 1824. The initials are those of Louis Philippe who had it taken to the Trianon. The cabinet work of the chest of drawers, which belonged to Charles X, is by Werner (1827) and the decorative bronze fittings are by Guillaume Deniere, one of the most important furniture suppliers to the Court in the time of Louis Philippe and Napoleon III. The laundry chests in Empire style, on either side the bed, bear the initials of Marie Amélie, consort of Louis Philippe, king of France.

In addition to the furnishings mentioned above, this room so full of historical memories, also contains fine Sèvres vases, noteworthy paintings and a magnificent carpet in clear colors.

It should be remembered that all the carpets are copies of antique originals which have been lost, except for the one from the Hall of Mirrors which is now in the French Embassy in Washington.

*The first anteroom or Salon des Seigneurs.*

*The vestibule on the side of the peristyle paved in black and white marble.*

**The Anteroom of the Chapel** - The name derives from the chapel that was installed in this room from 1687 on. The frieze below the cornice is decorated with ears of wheat and bunches of grapes to symbolize the bread and wine of the Communion. The altar faced the windows. In 1805 Napoleon had the chapel turned into a dining room for his mother and in 1810 it became the First Salon for Marie Louise and subsequently for the queen Marie Amélie.
Two large canvases represent the Evangelists Mark (above the mantelpiece) and Luke. The small round table (*guéridon*) in the center, decorated with the signs of the zodiac, was made by Martin for this room in 1811. The chairs are by Jacob-Desmalter and Marcion. The decoration of the room is completed by other paintings, fine vases and a golden yellow carpet.

**The First Antechamber** - Realized in 1692, in Louis XIV's time it was known as the Salon des Seigneurs. Like other rooms in the small palace it was subjected to various transformations and became the salon of Queen Marie Amélie's ushers in 1836.
The decoration of the walls is original and a motif of war trophies runs along the cornice. The fine painting over the fireplace is a reproduction of a painting by Mignard, executed by Delutel. It represents one of the

occupants of the Grand Trianon, the Grand Dauphin, son of Louis XIV, and his family: his wife Marie-Anne of Bavaria; the duke of Burgundy, on the right, was to be Louis XV's father, and the child seated on a cushion, the duke of Anjou, was to become king of Spain in 1700. Another child, the small Duc de Berry, is seated on his mother's lap. Like their father, all three children wear the large blue ribbon of the Order of the Holy Ghost, instituted by Henry III in 1578. To be noted are the portraits of Louis XV and Maria Leszczynska, copies after Van Loo, and a table with the tabletop made of one sole disk of teak 2.76 meters in diameter, the work of Félix Rémond (1823).
After visiting this room we cross the peristyle. When Napoleon lived here with his new consort, Marie Louise, the peristyle was closed with glass which was removed in 1910.
From here on to the left wing.

**The Round Room** - This antechamber has a magnificent floor of polychrome marble inlaid in geometric designs representing a star. Above the mantelpiece, a painting by Verdier of *Boreas Carrying Off Orithyia*. Another painting by the same artist represents *Juno and Thetis*. The overdoor decorations are by François Alexandre Desportes (1661-1743).

**The Officers' Room** - This hall was used as a Music Room after 1691. The doors of the musicians' loft can still be seen in the upper part of the wainscotting (*boiseries*). In Louis XV's time it was the king's antechamber and in the Napoleonic period it became the Officers' Room. Louis Philippe turned it into a billiard room.

The furnishings date from Napoleon's time and include the fine straight-back chairs and, in particular, the green bronze table with green Vosges granite tabletop. On a console, flanked by two gilded vases, is the curious clock in the form of Trajan's Column made in Sèvres biscuit and decorated with medallions of the signs of the zodiac. The samovar between two candelabra should also be noted.

**The Malachite Room** - Czar Alexander I presented Napoleon with the precious malachite used by Jacob Desmalter to make the tops of various pieces of furniture and a large basin for the Tuileries in 1809 which was installed here in 1811.

In Louis XIV's time it was the Cabinet du Couchant and is the only room in the Grand Trianon to have gilded wainscotting, executed in 1699 by Lassurance. The overdoor paintings, *Apollo and Thetis* and *Clytia Changed into a Heliotrope* by Charles de Lafosse, are of the same period. On the whole the furnishings are examples of Empire style. Also to be noted are the chairs by Jacob Desmalter and the piece of furniture in ebony and gilded bronze.

**The Salon Frais** - In Napoleon's time this room was used as a Council Chamber. Charles X held his last council of ministers here, in July 1830, before leaving for Rambouillet, on the way to exile.

The furnishings date to Napoleon's time: the document cabinet by Jacob-Desmalter, the stools upholstered in Beauvais tapestry, the precision clock and the thermometer. The paintings with views of Versailles are by J.B. Martin; above the fireplace, *Vertumnus and Pomona* by Bertin.

The *Room of the Springs* was named after the Garden of the Springs which no longer exists. It contains fine paintings by J.B. Martin, Chastelain, Houasse and the school of Monnoyer (for the paintings with floral themes).

*Below: The Officers' Room.*
*Facing page. Above: the Malachite Room with the fine basin made from the malachite sent to Napoleon by the czar of Russia. Below: the Salon Frais.*

*The Gallery.*

**The Gallery** - This long gallery built by Mansart preserves its original decoration. Eleven large doors that open out on the garden fill the interior with light. Simulated windows are decorated with compositions of children in bas-relief painted by François Lespingola (1644-1705). The stools and the consoles date to the First Empire. The crystal chandeliers were expressly made by the Moncenisio Factory.

The two tubs, *rafraichissoirs*, in marble from Languedoc, topped with a delightful decoration of ducks in the reeds, are from the time of Louis Philippe when the gallery was used as a dining room. These vases were made in 1750 for the Salle des Buffets.

The paintings between the windows representing the gardens of Versailles were commissioned by Louis XIV. In his 21 canvasses Jean Cotelle the Younger (1642-1708), portrait and miniature painter to the king, painted the palace gardens as they were in the 17th century. Mythological figures appear in some of the paintings. Etienne Allegrain (1644-1736), whose style is reminiscent of Nicolas Poussin, painted two other pictures. The last canvas by Jean Baptiste Martin, known as *Martin des Batailles* after he had received the official title of painter of the king's conquests in 1690. He also painted views of the palace and park of Versailles.

The palace and the gardens of Versailles seen from
the Bassin de Neptune, in a painting by Jean-Baptiste Martin
(1659-1753). In the distance, the Swiss lake
and the hills of Satory.

The Garden Room (Salon des Jardins).

Facing page: Napoleon's study.

**The Garden Room** - At the back of the Gallery is the *Garden Room* (*Salon des Jardins*) with a fine decoration by Lespingola. The walls are decorated with three paintings by Crépin: *Fishing, The Hunt*, and *The Stream*. As in the other rooms, the wooden floor is covered by a fine carpet. The chairs are in Empire style while the small round tables come from the dairy of the Petit Trianon. On the left, magnificent Japanese vases.

**Napoleon's Study** - Two rooms which are not always open to the public recall the great figure of Napoleon: his study and his bedroom. At the end of the Louis XIV reign this room was Madame de Maintenon's bedchamber and the pictures on the wall date to this period. The rest of the decoration is in Empire style. The large panels are green damask edged with guilded palmettes

and the upholstery on the chairs harmonize marvelously with the large carpet on the parquet floor.

The fireplace here is in typical Empire style although most of the fireplaces and mantelpieces in the palace of Versailles date of the time of Louise Philippe. The table top in polychrome marble stands on an Egyptian Revival base - a style characteristic of Napoleon's time. The document cabinet is by Jacob-Desmalter. Not to be overlooked are the porcelain vases and the clock on the mantelpiece which marked the Emperor's working hours.

Involved as Napoleon was from one end of the Empire to the other with all the valid men in the country in his wake, the time passed in this study must have been relatively limited, but even so what tales the walls would tell if they could speak.

*Facing page: Napoleon's chamber.*
*Above: a 17th-century view of the Grand Trianon.*

**Napoleon's chamber** - This is where Napoleon withdrew after his divorce in 1809. The wainscotting and the fireplace of Louis XV are still intact. The fine textiles of the bed and on the wall, in chamois colored moiré with borders in lilac and silver, had been woven for Josephine's room in the palace of the Tuileries. The emperor, forced to divorce by reasons of state, must have had melancholy thoughts in this room which reminded him of the happy moments he had spent here with his beloved Josephine. The furniture, from the emperor's living room, is in the style of the period. The desk was made by Baudouin while the bed and the chairs are by Jacob-Desmalter.

**Gardens of the Grand Trianon** - Retracing our steps through the Gallery, we go out to the gardens by Le Nôtre who modified what his nephew Le Bouteux had done. Two tubs enliven the pretty flowerbeds of the *Upper Garden*.
The *Lower Garden* provides a splendid panorama of the small arm of the *Plat-fond d'eau*, on the main axis of the palace. Shortly thereafter comes the fountain of the *Buffet d'eau* by Jules Hardouin Mansart (1703) with Neptune and Amphitrite at its summit.
The gardens of the Grand Trianon, which differ greatly from those of Versailles, are just the place to go when in the mood for poetry.

# THE PETIT TRIANON

Louis XV detested the etiquette his great grandfather, the Sun King, had imposed on the court. It was the Marquise de Pompadour who thought of building a smaller château near the Botanical Gardens of the Grand Trianon to give the king a place where he could relax away from Versailles. The setting for a bucolic life was supplied by building a farm, with a new parterre, the French Garden, and in 1750 Gabriel added a pavilion in fine white stone. The French Pavilion was a large oval room flanked by four small rooms. Of a marvelously classic taste, the exterior has a facade in smooth ashlars and consists of a single story crowned by a balustrade supporting large vases and sculptures of putti. This peaceful corner was not meant to be lived in but was used for picnics or to pass an hour of diversion. It was then that Jacques Ange Gabriel planned a new château, the Petit Trianon.

The architect had already designed buildings and city plans in Choisy, Fontainebleau, Marly, and was to demonstrate his talent once more with the building of the Petit Trianon, the Salon dell'Opéra in Versailles and the square dedicated to Louis XV, the future Place de la Concorde.
Surrounded by greenery, this elegant building with its pure lines was built in two years, between 1762 and 1764, and another four years were needed to complete the interior decoration.
Madame de Pompadour died in April 1764 and never lived in this "refuge" she had thought up for her royal lover. Louis XV rarely went to the Petit Trianon, under stress because of the political mood and pained by numerous deaths in the family - that of the Dauphin, in 1765, followed by that of the queen three years later. In 1770 the court came back to life with

the arrival of Marie Antoinette, grand duchess of Austria and bride of the heir to the throne. This charming 15-year-old girl loved to enjoy herself, and the king, already in his sixties, took a benevolent attitude with regards to the girl and her young husband who had just turned 16 and was still rather awkward but who one day was to become the 63rd king of France. Occasionally ths idyllic family picture was troubled by the tensions provoked by Choiseul and the Comtesse du Barry, the king's new favorite, and their retinue.
On May 10, 1774, the fateful "The king is dead. Long live the king!" resounded through the halls. The young Marie Antoinette, queen at nineteen, who loved flowers and simplicity, was soon to receive the Petit Trianon as a gift and was to transform it in the fashion then in vogue, in other words following her own personal taste.

Facing page. Above: the Grand Salon or the Music Room.
Below: anteroom with wainscotting from the time
of Louis XV and the "grandfather" clock.

View of the dining room. On the mantelpiece,
a bust of the queen, Marie Antoinette.

**The exterior** - The entrance gate is flanked on either side by a sentry box decorated with an oval window opening ornamented with a garland of flowers. At the back of the courtyard is a three-storied square building with a ground floor in rusticated ashlar, an intermediate floor and an attic crowned by a balustrade. The four engaged pilasters rhythmically accent the verticality of the large windows on the first floor. The southwestern facade overlooking the French Garden has no basement, nor does the northeast facade, due to the uneveness of the terrain and has a portico consisting of four Corinthian columns.

**The interior** - The entrance hall is on the same level as the staircase which has a fine railing, a real masterpiece of 18th-century wrought iron, decorated with the queen's initials. The lantern dates to the same period but was installed later by the empress Marie Louise. The ground floor consists of a guard room, the kitchens which Marie Antoinette had changed into pantries in 1781, a storeroom, a room for silver, and a

billiard room up until 1784. The first floor has an antechamber decorated with wainscotting made by Jacques Verberckt in 1750 for a pavilion that was later demolished. The furnishing of this lovely room is completed by the beautiful corner cupboard by Riesener and a splendid "grandfather" clock made in 1787 by Robin, clockmaker to the king. On either side, the window busts of Louis XVI and Joseph II, Marie Antoinette's brother. The dining room, transformed by the queen, now once more looks as it did when Guibert designed it in Louis XV's time. The light green of the wood panelling, the gilded garlands and the paintings lend the room a unique charm. Above the doors are *Agriculture* by Lagrenée, *The Hunt* by Joseph Marie Vien (1716-1809), *Fishing* by Gabriel François Boyen (1726-1806) and *The Vintage* by Noël Hallé (1711-1781). The sideboards in mahogany with superb fittings in bronze are attributed to Martin Carlin (1730-1785), a French cabinetmaker trained in Œben's atelier (1710-1763) like his famous contemporaries Riesener and Leleu. The chairs, examples of Louis XV

121

The queen's boudoir, once equipped with sliding mirrors
which could shut out the outside.
The exquisitely made objects are in keeping
with Marie Antoinette's taste.

style, have straight rectangular backs and round grooved legs with the typical join consisting of a cube decorated with a rosette. They were made by Jean-Baptiste-Claude Séné, famous French 18th-century *ébéniste*. Originally they were not part of the furnishings of the Petit Trianon. To be noted also an ostrich egg mounted on an ivory base, made by Jean-Etienne Lebel for Madame Adelaïde, and two eggs mounted in white box-wood and ebony from the collections of the Crown. Next to the dining room is the drawing room in Louis XV style, transformed by Marie Antoinette into a billiard room. Outstanding the chest of drawers by Riesener and the arm-chairs.

Next comes *the queen's chamber*. The furniture with its "*Aux Epis*" decoration of ears of wheat was delivered by Jacob two years before the Revolution. The textiles are authentic. The commode is by Riesener. The famous portrait of the Dauphin painted by Kucharski is in the dressing room. The dressing table is by Riesener and the ivory time-piece was made by Louis XVI himself for the queen. The Grand Salon, known also as the Music Room, is one of the loveliest in the Petit Trianon. Marie Antoinette was extremely fond of music and Grétry was her teacher. Her favorite instruments were the harp and the harpsichord. When the furniture was recently restored it was upholstered in a lovely three-color damask. The writing table is by Riesener, the chairs by Séné.

On August 25, 1793, a public ball was held on the occasion of the auctioning off of the objects which had belonged to the queen. Subsequently the Directory hired out the Petit Trianon to a certain Langlos, a lemonade vender, who transformed it into a public dance hall and also installed swings. Napoleon had his sister Pauline Borghese stay there and then turned it over to the empress Marie Louise, niece of Marie Antoinette. Finally, in 1867 the empress Eugénie collected various objects which had belonged to Marie Antoinette in this small château which she had so dearly loved. These first attempts were to be followed up by others and the Petit Trianon once more became part of history.

# THE QUEEN'S THEATER

Marie Antoinette was fascinated by the theater. As early as 1776 a provisory auditorium had been set up in the old Orangerie, behind the Petit Trianon, but it no longer exists.

Two years later, in the month of June, work began on the construction of a small theater and a year later it was finished. The first plays were not given until 1780. The company of actors included various members of the royal Family and their Friends Representations were rigorously reserved for the family and the following. The queen herself appeared on stage a dozen times, interpreting comic roles of servant, maid or milkmaid. On August 19, 1785, she played the part of Rosina in the *Barber of Seville* by Beaumarchais, with music by Paisiello, and with Comte d'Artois, the future king Charles X, in the part of Figaro. The author personally directed rehearsals and watched the play seated next to the king.

Outside, the building is quite modest and only the entrance portal has two Ionic columns with a triangular tympanum containing the *Child Apollo with a Lyre*, by Deschamps. The four bas-reliefs in the atrium, also by Deschamps, represent the Muses. Their facial expressions are particularly charming and the figures move with exceptional grace and harmony.

The interior in blue and gold is sumptuously decorated. The monogram of the queen appears in the cartouche of the vaulted ceiling, held up by two figures emanating rays. The ceiling painted by Legrange no longer exists. We know that it represented Apollo surrounded by the Graces and the Muses. On either side of the stage with its gold-fringed blue curtain is a candelabrum formed of female figures with a horn of plenty, in gilded papier-mâché. From 1785 on, the health of the Dauphin gradually worsened and the mood of the court became gloomy. Balls were no longer given and the queen closed her theater. The representatives of the provinces of the kingdom who came to the meeting of the States General on May 5, 1789, requested to visit the Trianon and the theater, expecting to discover who knows what ostentation and luxury, a supposition cleverly fanned by a denigratory newspaper campaign. But they went home deluded because the decoration they thought would be "all diamonds" turned out to be a simple stage set with a few sequins scattered here and there.

# THE GARDEN

*"Aimable Trianon que de transports divers*
*Vous inspirez aux âmes amoureuses!*
*J'ai cru voir en entrant sous vos ombrages verts*
*Le séjour des ombres heureuses".*

These were the words of Antoine de Bertin, known as the "French Propertius" for the lyricism of his elegiacal verses. This sweet mood may be ours too as we wander through the park where nature seems to do her best to outdo man in elegance, secluded from the crowded avenues of the palace. Every corner seems to be the site of one of Watteau's airy compositions. And in the end our wanderings inevitably lead us to the Temple of Love which Marie Antoinette could see from her chamber.

Richard Mique built the small temple in just a few months, with a circular base of six fine stone steps on which rest twelve grooved Corinthian columns which sustain a coffered dome. Under the dome is *Cupid Carving his Darts from the Club of Hercules*, a marble copy by Louis Philippe Mouchy of the original by Bouchardon which is in the Museum of the Louvre. All around, the gardener planted ornamental apple trees, roses, flower beds, and a large umbrella willow in homage to the romanticism of the spot. For some of the fetes, the temple was illuminated at night and hundreds of bundles of kindling wood were burned in the pits expressly dug behind the building. Continuing our walk we reach the hamlet (*Hameau*), at present consisting of nine buildings: the Queen's House, the Billiard House, the Food-warming House, the Boudoir, the Mill, the Guard's House, the Dovecote, Marlborough Tower and the Dairy; the Ballroom and the Cheese Factory have disappeared. Marlborough Tower rises on the other side of the pond, facing the Mill and the Queen's

*Below: the Temple of Love.*
*Facing page: the hamlet and the Mill.*

*Illumination of the Belvedere of the Petit Trianon
on July 26, 1781, during a fete in honor of
the Comte de Provence, future King Louis XVIII.
Painting by Claude-Louis Chatelet (1753-1794).*

House. The building was used as an observatory on top and for fishing below. The name derives from the song "Marlborough s'en va-t-en guerre" which Madame Poitrine, the Dauphin's nurse, sang as a lullaby to the royal infant.

A bucolic life animated these places and the farm produced milk, cheese and eggs and was filled with the sound of clucking hens, mooing cattle, cooing pigeons and the bleating of the ten nanny goats and the billy goat the queen wanted "...white and tame...".

A lovely building, the *Belvedere*, rises on a small promontory overlooking the lake, near the Rock and the Mountain of the Snail. Surrounded by eight sphinxes this pleasant look-out has a charm all its own. Fine bas-reliefs by Deschamps representing the Four Seasons are set above the windows. Over the doors a frieze of tendrils and a tympanum sculptured with rustic trophies. A delicate frieze of flowers, fruits and ribbons runs along under the crowning of the building. Inside, the painted stucco, with horns, vases, animals, bird cages and the ever-present bouquets tied with ribbons, is by Le Riche. It is said the queen loved to have her breakfast here.

Not far from the Belvedere is the grotto in which Marie Antoinette was quietly reading on that fateful 5th of October, 1789, when a breathless page came running up with a letter from the minister of the royal house communicating that a group of armed rioters were marching on Versailles.

She was never again to see her beloved flowers, her beribboned lambs, nor her "tame white" billy goat and she would courageously face the birth of a new era.

# KINGS, QUEENS AND MISTRESSES IN VERSAILLES

**LOUIS XIV**
(1638 - 1715)
*king 1643 - 1715*

**MARIE THERESE OF AUSTRIA**
(1638-1683)
⊞*1660*

**FRANÇOISE D'AUBIGNÉ**
marquise de Maintenon
(1635-1719)
*morganatic wife
from 1685*

**FRANÇOISE LOUISE DE LA BAUME LE BLANC**
duchesse de La Vallière
(1644-1710)
*mistress*

**FRANÇOISE ATHÉNAÏS DE ROCHECHOUART DE MORTEMART**
marquise de Montespan
(1641-1707)
*mistress*

LOUIS
le Grand Dauphin (1661-1711)

LOUIS
duc de Bourgogne
(1682-1712)

LOUIS
(1704-1705)

LOUIS
duc de Bretagne
(1707-1712)

**LOUIS XV**
(1710-1774)
*king 1715-74*

**MARIA LESZCZYŃSKA**
(1703-1768)
⊞*1725*

**JEANNE ANTOINETTE POISSON**
marquise de
Pompadour
(1721-1764)
*mistress*

**MARIE JEANNE BÉCU**
comtesse du Barry
(1746-1793)
*mistress*

LOUIS
Dauphin
(1729-1765)

MARIE-JOSÈPHE OF SAXONY
(1731-1767)

LOUISE-ELISABETH (1727-1759)
HENRIETTE (1727-1752)
ADÉLAÏDE (1732-1800)
VICTOIRE (1733-1799)
SOPHIE (1734-1782)
LOUISE (1737-1787)

**LOUIS XVI**
(1754-1793)
*king 1774-92*

**MARIE ANTOINETTE OF AUSTRIA**
(1755-1793)
⊞*1770*

**LOUIS XVII**
(1785-1795)
*king 1793-95*

**LOUIS XVIII**
(1755-1824)
*king 1814-24*

**MARIE-JOSÈPHE-LOUISE OF SAVOY**
(1753-1810)
⊞*1771*

**CHARLES X**
(1757-1836)
*king 1824-1830
(abdicated)*

**MARIA THERESA OF SAVOY**
(1756-1805)
⊞*1773*

# TABLE OF CONTENTS

*All rights reserved. No part of this book may be reproduced without the written permission of the Publisher.*
*The cover, layout and artwork by the Casa Editrice Bonechi graphic artists*
*in this publication are protected by international copyright.*
*Printed in Italy by* Centro Stampa Editoriale Bonechi.
*Translated by* Erika Pauli.
Diffusion: OVET-PARIS - 13, rue des Nanettes - 75011 Paris - Tel. 43 38 56 80
We wish to thank the *Réunion des Musées Nationaux* for the photographs on pages 24, 38, 59 and 127

ISBN 88-7009-375-1

* * *